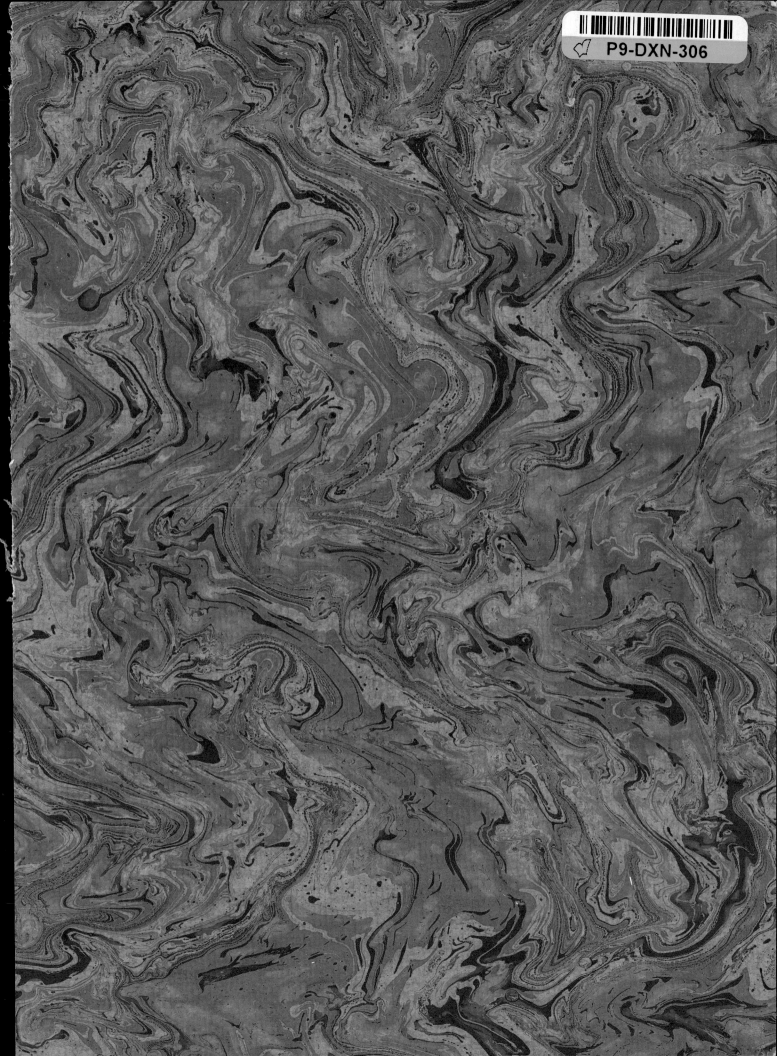

Selections from the DECORATIVE ARTS in the J. Paul Getty Museum

Selections from the

DECORATIVE ARTS

in the J. Paul Getty Museum

Gillian Wilson

THE J. PAUL GETTY MUSEUM
MALIBU · CALIFORNIA

© 1983 The J. Paul Getty Museum
17985 Pacific Coast Highway
Malibu, California 90265
(For further information about museum books,
please write Bookstore, The J. Paul Getty Museum,
P.O. Box 2112, Santa Monica, California 90406)

Library of Congress catalogue number 82-681807
ISBN number 0-89236-037-2 (hardbound)
            0-89236-050-x (paperbound)

Library of Congress Cataloging in Publication Data
J. Paul Getty Museum.
    Selections from the collection of decorative arts
in the J. Paul Getty Museum.

    Bibliography: p.
    Includes index.
    1. Decorative arts—France—History—17th century.
2. Decorative arts—France—History—18th century.
3. Decorative arts—France—History—19th century.
4. Decorative arts—California—Malibu. 5. J. Paul
Getty Museum. I. Wilson, Gillian
II. Title.
NK947.J2 1983   745'.0944   82-681807

Photography by Donald Hull and Penelope Potter
Design by COY, Los Angeles
Typography by Andresen Typographics, Los Angeles
Printed by Alan Lithograph, Inc.
Bound by Roswell Bookbinders Phoenix, Arizona
in an edition of 5000 copies.

TABLE OF CONTENTS

ACKNOWLEDGMENTS

The texts for Nos. 26, 28, 29, 33, 40, 48, and 49 were written by Adrian Sassoon. I am grateful to the following people for various items of information used in compiling this book: Geoffrey de Bellaigue, Andrew Ciechanowiecki, David Cohen, Theodore Dell, Anthony Derham, Svend Ericksen, Roland de l'Espée, Ronald Freyberger, Arthur Grimwade, Leslie Harris, Henry Hawley, Guy Kuraszewski, Bozenna Majewska-Maszkowska, James Parker, Alexandre Pradère, Tamara Préaud, Olga Raggio, Rosalind Savill, Edith Standen, Pierre Verlet, and Sir Francis Watson. I am especially indebted to Colin Streeter who read the manuscript and made many useful suggestions and essential corrections.

INTRODUCTION

J. Paul Getty began to collect French decorative arts in the 1930's and continued to do so until his death in 1976. In the early 1970's the collection began to expand at a rapid pace, and this rate of expansion has continued relatively unabated until the present. At least half of the objects illustrated here have been acquired since Mr. Getty's death.

The collection, at the time that this book is published, contains over three hundred individual pieces; this volume illustrates fifty of them. The objects have been chosen to represent a cross section of the collection, which extends from approximately 1660 to 1820. It covers the reigns of Louis XIV, Louis XV, and Louis XVI and is now beginning to include objects made during the Empire under Napoleon.

This book is not a catalogue (which is now in preparation), nor is it a mere picture book or checklist. Each piece has been chosen and illustrated because it represents a particular aspect of the crafts involved in the production of objects that were, in the main, made for the crown, the nobility, and the rich bourgeoisie of Paris. In addition to furniture, the book includes clocks, tapestries, porcelains, and objects made solely of gilded bronze, and silver. The pieces are arranged in chronological order. Translations of the French archival extracts, an index, and a concise bibliography for further reading have been provided.

This carpet was probably made in the workshops of Philippe Lourdet in the mid-seventeenth century. Philippe's father, Simon Lourdet, started his career as a Louvre workshop apprentice, then went into business on his own in the Savonnerie, an old soap factory at Chaillot. From 1672 the Savonnerie manufactory, under the direction of the court painter Charles Le Brun, and at the order of the minister Jean-Baptiste Colbert, worked only for the Crown. This carpet therefore predates the extremely elaborate productions made for the Château de Versailles and the Palais du Louvre. It has a close affinity to the oriental carpets which predominate in the inventories of Louis XIV.

In the center of this large carpet is a sunflower, the symbol of the self-styled Sun King, Louis XIV (1643–1715). Around the border are images of flower-filled Chinese porcelain bowls of the Ming period — an early representation of oriental objects on French work. In the inventory of Louix XIV we find the following entry:

No. l8. Un grand tapis neuf de la Savonnerie fonds brun, parsemé de grands rinseaux blancs et de fleurs au naturel, ayant au milieu un cartouche ovalle dans lequel il y a un feston de fleurs avec un tournesol au milieu dudit feston, dans une bordure aussy fonds brun avec des corbeilles et vases de fleurs, Long de sept aunes ½, large de trois aunes ⅔.

This description, apart from the size and the brown ground color, corresponds to the museum's carpet. It is likely that the compiler of the inventory made a mistake over the ground color, as all known carpets of this design have a dark-blue ground. The difference in size can be explained by the fact that the carpet has been cut down at its shorter sides by some two feet and only the borders carefully replaced in the late nineteenth century. Nevertheless, it is not certain that this carpet is the one listed in Louis XIV's inventory, as other carpets of similar design and size exist, notably at the Château de Vaux-le-Vicomte.

The museum's carpet is remarkable for its fine state of preservation. It is almost completely unworn and retains its bright colors. One half of the carpet is illustrated.

French (Savonnerie); c. 1640–1660

Length: 21′ 9″ (668.1 cm.)
Breadth: 14′ 4″ (439.5 cm.)

Accession number 70.DC.63

Woolen knots on a linen weft and warp.

At various times in the late seventeenth and early eighteenth centuries, items of silver were melted down at the order of Louis XIV to help defray the cost of the punishingly expensive wars that France was constantly waging against its neighbors. For this reason, very little French silver of the period exists today. The survival of this fountain is due to the fact that it was sent to England shortly after its manufacture, by 1698 at the latest, when an exact copy of it was made by Ralph Leeke, who also made two cisterns en suite. The fountain (like its copy, which was last seen in the 1940's) bears the arms of Sir Nathaniel Curzon, 1st Baron Scarsdale, and his wife Caroline Colyear, the daughter of the 2nd Earl of Portmore, who were married in 1750. It is not known when the fountain came into Scarsdale's possession. Both the fountains and the cisterns may have been acquired by Sir Nathaniel after his inheritance in 1758; he is known to have invested heavily in silver and paintings soon afterwards. A bill survives, dated 1759, for the cost of re-engraving the arms on all four pieces.

The architect Robert Adam was employed in the 1760's to provide neoclassical interiors for Curzon's country seat, Kedleston Hall. Drawings by Adam exist of the niche in the dining room showing a sideboard arrangement with the fountains and cisterns in place. Drawings of the fountain alone also exist. It is possible that, in its original form, before it left France, the fountain was a vase with one large handle, of the type seen in early Gobelins tapestries such as the series known as the *Maisons Royales*. It may well have been converted into a fountain by Ralph Leeke, and it seems likely that the foot, with its classical Greek key, was a later replacement to make the fountain fit more appropriately into Adams's neoclassical interior at Kedleston.

The fountain is stamped with the date letter R beneath a crown for 1661 and with the maker's mark ⚜, which is not recorded. It has been suggested that the prominent scepter with its fleur-de-lys, seen between the letters, may indicate that it is the mark of an *orfèvre-du-roi* working in the Louvre. Such an imposing vessel may well have been made for the King, and it is possible that it was made as a royal gift to some member of the English court.

One of the Scarsdale cisterns is now in the collection of the Goldsmiths' Hall, London; the other is in the Victoria and Albert Museum.

French (Paris); c. 1661

Height: 2' 1⅝" (65.2 cm.)
Width: 1' 2⅛" (35.9 cm.)
Depth: 1' 2¼" (36.2 cm.)

Accession number 82.DG.17

Silver.

This elaborate cabinet was probably made at the Gobelins Manufactory, which was set up in 1662 by Jean-Baptiste Colbert to make furnishings for the royal châteaux and palaces. The decorative scheme on the cabinet refers to Louix XIV's military victories: the central door is decorated with a panel of marquetry showing the cockerel of France standing triumphant over the lion of Spain and the eagle of the Austrian Empire. Between 1672 and 1678 France was indeed triumphant over these two countries, and a temporary peace was secured by the signing of the Treaty of Nijmegen in 1678.

The cabinet is supported by carved wooden figures representing Hercules and perhaps his consort Omphale. Below the cornice are bronze mounts of military trophies, framing a medallion of Louis XIV.

The pair to the cabinet belongs to the Duke of Buccleuch and stands in his Scottish country seat, Drumlanrig Castle. The early provenance of these two cabinets is not known, but it is possible that they were brought to Britain in the early decades of the nineteenth century. The museum's cabinet was formerly in the possession of the Earls of Dudley, and it is known that by 1900 it stood in one of their houses, Witley Court. No trace of the cabinets has been found in the French royal archives, nor is it known precisely where they were made. Objects of such grandeur were usually produced at the Gobelins workshops, but it is possible that the cabinets were made by the royal cabinetmaker André-Charles Boulle in his workshop at the Louvre.

The presence of fleurs-de-lys on the cornice indicates that the cabinets were made for the Crown, or at least at the King's command, but they do not appear in Louis XIV's inventories. Nevertheless, the Sun King's portrait appears twice on the cabinet. The medallion above the door, which was cast from one made by Jean Varin in 1659, shows the King at the age of twenty-one. Inside is another medallion, also taken from a medal by Varin, which shows the King at the age of twenty-five.

French (Gobelins?);
c. 1670–1680

Height: 7' 5" (226.7 cm.)
Width: 4' 5" (134.6 cm.)
Depth: 2' 1½" (64.8 cm.)

Accession number 77.DA.1

Veneered with tortoiseshell, brass, pewter, ivory, ebony, with stained and natural woods, set with bronze mounts. The figures are of oak, painted and gilded.

4. TABLE

The surface of the table top is centered by a large oval of tortoiseshell, inlaid with brass at its outer edge and surrounded by a frame of naturalistic flowers in wood marquetry. Peonies, hyacinths, daffodils, tulips, and ranunculus can be identified. Four bearded masks, also in wood marquetry, appear at the corners. The legs are veneered with horn painted to resemble tortoiseshell and inlaid with finely engraved pewter. Four small birds on the surface are identical to four found on the drawer fronts of the cabinet illustrated as No. 3. It is therefore reasonable to assume that the marquetry on both pieces is by the same hand, but whether the hands belonged to some as yet unidentified worker at the Gobelins Manufactory or to André-Charles Boulle, the royal cabinetmaker working at the Louvre, is still not known. If we turn to the inventory of Louis XIV, a number of similar tables are described:

No. 122. Une table fond d'ébeine, à compartimens de bois blanc, en forme d'un jonc de feüilles de chesne, toute couverte de marqueterie de fleurs et oyseaux de bois de diverses couleurs, les bases et chapiteaux du pied de cuivre doré.

Nos. 162,163. Deux tables d'escaille de tortue, à compartimens de fleurs et oyseaux de marqueterie de bois de diverses couleurs au naturel, profilez d'yvoire, avec leur pieds à colonnes, dont les bazes, astragales et chapiteaux sont cuivre doré........

Most of the tables listed in Louis XIV's inventory include the use of ivory and have straight legs. The museum's table has only three small ivory flowers on the stretcher, and the legs are elaborately scrolled. Three tables that can be closely compared to it exist. One was formerly at Warwick Castle; a second, formerly in the possession of Madame Polès, passed through the art market in 1979; and the third is in the museum's collection. Few pieces decorated in this fragile manner have survived, and it is likely that most of the tables in Louis XIV's inventory were destroyed in the course of time.

It should be recognized that this table once had a very bright appearance. The wood marquetry flowers would have been more strongly colored, and some of the horn was originally painted bright blue behind, though it has now faded to a uniform gray.

The table, like the cabinet in No. 3, was once in the possession of the Earls of Dudley.

French (Gobelins?);
c. 1670–1680

Height: 2′ 4½″ (72.4 cm.)
Width: 3′ 8½″ (112.4 cm.)
Depth: 2′ 6½″ (77.5 cm.)

Accession number
71.DA.100

Veneered with brass, pewter, tortoiseshell, horn, ebony, and ivory, with stained and natural woods.

9

5. TABLE

This small table is veneered, in the main, with pewter, brass, and tortoiseshell. The ground, or background, of the design is of pewter, with the major decorative elements in tortoiseshell; this form of decoration is known as *contre partie*. It is a pair to a table in the British Royal Collection, where the materials forming the veneer are reversed, the ground being of shell and the design elements in metal. This, the more familiar technique, is known as *première partie*.

The table opens to reveal a central oval scene in pewter, brass, shell, ebony, and wood of three Chinese figures taking tea under a tent with a large baldachin, surrounded by trees in which perch a monkey and a parrot. It seems likely that the table may have never been restored (indeed, it was almost completely black when it appeared on the market), as even the engraving in the tortoiseshell remains intact. On most objects decorated in this manner, the engraving in the relatively soft shell is usually abraded and lost.

It is probable that the table was made for the Grand Dauphin (1661–1711). It bears on the frieze and on the stand four prominent fleurs-de-lys and, on the folding-out flaps, large scaly tortoiseshell dolphins, the emblem of the Dauphin. It is known that the renowned cabinetmaker André-Charles Boulle provided furniture decorated in brass, tortoiseshell, and pewter for the Dauphin; indeed, he created a small room in this technique for Louis XIV's eldest son. But, as is usually the case with objects made in this technique, the lack of documents makes it impossible to support a firm attribution to this master. It is known that it was not just Boulle who worked in this florid technique, and it has been suggested that the table may be the work of a lesser-known craftsman who worked at the Manufacture Royale at the Gobelins, Pierre Golle. A few works may be quite safely attributed to this maker, and the design and cutting of the marquetry does resemble his work.

The pair to this table was illustrated in Pyne's *Royal Residences* in 1819, when it stood in the Queen's Presence Chamber at Windsor Castle. It is possible that the museum's table was in Britain by this date, but it is not known when these small tables left France. The table in the Royal Collection has been traditionally called a piquet table, piquet being a popular card game in the second half of the seventeenth century. This seems an unlikely use, as the decoration on the top would easily be caught and lifted by the action of the cards. It seems more likely that the table was intended to hold a tray with tea bowls—following the theme of the decoration.

French (Paris); c. 1675–1680

Height: 2' 6" (76 cm.)
Width (closed):
1' 2½" (37 cm.),
(open):
2' 4½" (72.5 cm.)
Depth: 1' 4½" (42 cm.)

Accession number
82.DA.34

Wood veneered with tortoiseshell, pewter, brass and ebony, mounted with gilt bronze and with gilt gessoed wood.

11

These coffers on stands, one of which is illustrated, have long been associated with the marriage of the Grand Dauphin in 1680. The coffers have been discussed in numerous publications since their first appearance in recent history at the sale of Prince Demidoff in 1880. Almost without exception, furniture historians have attributed them to the workshop of André-Charles Boulle (1642-1732), the perfecter of the style of marquetry with which these coffers are decorated — incorporating tortoiseshell, brass, pewter, and ebony.

We know from an unpublished manuscript of the Grand Dauphin's inventory that Boulle did provide him with a similar coffer:

6. Un cabinet de marqueterie en forme de tombeau dont le fond est d'écaille de tortue, de cuivre jaune et d'estain, garni de six bandes canelées de cuivre doré ornées par le haut de testes de femmes et par le bas de mufles de lions, haut de trois pieds neuf pouces, long de sieze pouces onze lignes et large de treize pouces. Fait par Boulle.

However, the description and size do not fit the museum's coffers exactly: only one is mentioned, not two, and this single coffer apparently did not possess a stand. But the inventory description is close enough to allow a fairly firm attribution to Boulle for the museum's coffers. It is almost certain that the stands are contemporary and were made for the coffers. All the gilt bronze mounts are stamped with the tax stamp of the crowned C, showing that the coffers were with the stands in the last years of the 1740's when the tax on copper was enforced (see p. 38). We know that a coffer *en tombeau* on a stand, both of apparently the same form as 82.DA.109.1, was sold, with a lengthy description, from the collection of C.-F. Julliot in 1777.

One of the stands closely follows a drawing attributed to A.-C. Boulle in the Musée des Arts Décoratifs, Paris, where it is shown supporting a rectangular cabinet.

In the Demidoff sale, the coffers and stands are illustrated in engravings, where they appear precisely as they do today. Since 1880 they have had a number of owners, one being the American heiress Anna Gould who became the duchesse de Talleyrand.

French; c. 1680

Height (of coffers):
2' 2⅜" (60.7 cm.);
Width: 2' 11½" (89.9 cm.)
Depth: 1' 10" (55.8 cm.)
Height (of stands):
2' 11½" (89.6 cm.)
Width: 2' 7½" (80 cm.)
Depth: 1' 9" (54 cm.)

Accession number
82.DA.109.1-2

Oak veneered with ebony, pewter, brass, and tortoise-shell, with gilt bronze mounts.

13

The name of the maker of this terra cotta model for a clock is not known, but in its fine yet freely modeled details we surely see the hand of an accomplished sculptor. The group of Pluto and Persephone in a chariot drawn by four horses recalls the work of François Girardon (1628-1715), while the vigorously modeled winged dragons perched on the scrolled legs are far in advance of the rather static bronzes found on other clocks of this date.

The model is full size, and set into the face, which is decorated with Berainesque motifs, are enamel numbers, two of which have been slightly ground down to accomodate the winding holes — a detail which may indicate that the model was subsequently adapted to take a movement. That an object made of this fragile material has survived at all is a rarity, and there are some small losses. The vases at the four upper corners have lost their contents; and the figure on the top, which may have been Father Time seated with a globe or a figure representing Fame, is missing.

No clocks bearing Pluto and Persephone beneath the face are known, but a clock described as follows was sold at the auction house of Christie's in 1899:

Lot 48. A Louis XIV bracket clock, in scroll shaped Boulle case mounted with Pluto and Persephone, and other chasing, and borders of or-moulu, and surmounted by a figure of Fame and bracket en suite. 50 ins high.

Miniature models, usually made of wax or terra cotta with painted paper, were sometimes produced for royal commissions, but few have survived. A model for a jewel cabinet made for Marie-Antoinette about 1770 is in the Walters Art Gallery, Baltimore, and a small wax chair is in a French private collection. The chair has arms and legs of differing designs and was made for Marie-Antoinette by Charles Gondouin as a proposal for a set of seat furniture for the *Salon du Rocher* at the Petit Trianon. The museum's clock, however, is the earliest known Parisian model for a piece of furniture.

French (Paris); c. 1700-1710

Height: 2' 7" (78.7 cm.)
Width: 1' 8½" (52.1 cm.)
Depth: 9½" (24.1 cm.)

Accession number
72.DB.52

Terra cotta and enamel.

This tapestry, known as a *Char de Triomphe*, was woven at the Gobelins manufactory following cartoons prepared by the decorative painter Baudrain Yvart *le père* (1611-1690), after designs by Charles le Brun.

The original cartoon was painted in 1659-1660 at the order of Nicolas Fouquet (1615-1680), the infamous finance minister who was imprisoned by Louis XIV in 1661. He was the builder of the Château de Vaux-le-Vicomte and had established his own tapestry works at the village of Maincy nearby. At the fall of Fouquet, Colbert moved the looms, workers, and cartoons to the Manufacture Royale des Gobelins.

Sixty-six tapestries were woven from the *Char de Triomphe* cartoon, in which the arms of Fouquet, incorporating a squirrel, were replaced with the arms of France and Navarre. The first came from the looms in 1691 and the last, in 1724. Twelve of the tapestries were woven with gold thread, and those were burnt in 1797 after the Revolution to retrieve the precious metal. The museum's tapestry bears the inventory number 194 painted on its lining. The number can be traced in the Inventory of the Garde Meuble de la Couronne, where it is recorded that the tapestry was one of four delivered on the 27th October 1717 for the use of Louis XIV. The entry reads as follows:

No. 194: Portières du char: Quatre portières de tapisserie de basse lisse, laine et soie, manufacture des Gobelins, dessein de Le Brun, représentant au milieu les armes et la devise de Louis XIV dans un cartouche porté sur un Char de Triomphe, accompagné de trophées d'armes; la bordure est un guillochis qui enferme des fleurs de lys et des roses couleur de bronze; chaque portière contient 2 aunes ½ cours sur 2 aunes ⅚ de haut.

For a tapestry of this date, it is in quite remarkable condition both in its fabric and its color.

French (Gobelins); 1717

Height: 11' 5" (350 cm.)
Width: 9' 2" (280 cm.)

Accession number
83.DD.20

Silk and wool.

17

The corners of the clock are mounted with four male figures of gilt bronze, emblematic of the four continents: Asia, Africa, America, and Europe. The case is veneered with tortoiseshell and brass. The pedestal is also veneered with tortoiseshell, and on the front is a large medallion of gilt bronze showing Hercules relieving Atlas of the weight of the Heavens.

The most unusual feature of the clock is its oval face. To facilitate reading the time, the hour hand is formed of two overlapping sections, the outer one fitting onto an oval gilt bronze molding. As the hour hand travels around the face, it expands and contracts, being shortest at three and nine o'clock and longest at six and twelve o'clock. The complicated mechanism was made by Julien Le Roy (master in 1713), whose name is found inscribed on the back plate of the movement and also painted on the small enamel plaque below the face. It is not known who made the case, but the quality of its construction and the extremely finely cast and chased mounts point to the royal cabinetmaker André-Charles Boulle.

Four other clocks of this model are known. One is in the James A. de Rothschild Collection at Waddesdon Manor, and another is in the Wallace Collection, London. Both now have circular faces and later movements, the former by George Graham and the latter by Myneul. A third clock, in the Bibliothèque de l'Arsenal in Paris, still has its oval face. Its movement is signed by Gilles Martinot, while the plaque below, strangely, is painted "Julien LeRoy." A fourth clock, recently discovered in a Norwegian collection, has an oval face but a normal hour hand in one piece. The enamel plaque below is painted "Julien LeRoy," while the movement itself is not inscribed.

The museum's clock represents a high point in the development of French clocks both in the technical supremacy of its movement and the extremely high quality of the case. Interestingly, a long case clock in the collection (accession number 72.DB.40) of about the same date bears the same four figures representing the continents; but in this instance they are clumsily cast and not well chased. They are obviously made from the same models but by a less able *bronzier.*

French (Paris); c. 1715-1720

Height: 10′ 9⅜″ (335 cm.)
Width: 2′ 3⅜″ (69.6 cm.)
Depth: 1′ 2″ (35.5 cm.)

Accession number 74.DB.1

Veneered with tortoiseshell, ebony, and brass, set with gilt bronze mounts, enamel numbers and plaque.

19

Large tables such as this were known as *bureaux plats*. The model illustrated here was a fairly common one: other examples are also found veneered with "boulle" marquetry of tortoiseshell and brass. The tables were often provided with a *cartonnier* and its *serre papier*, that stood at one end. The surface would originally have been covered with short-piled velvet or velour; the fashion for recovering with leather began in the nineteenth century, and the easily damaged fabric is rarely seen on table tops today.

The gilt bronze mounts of the museum's table are of exceptionally fine quality and are heavily gilded. The model has been attributed to the cabinetmaker Charles Cressent (1685-1768), but no tables of this description are to be found in the many documents that describe the contents of his workshop, nor does the design of the table relate to any of his known works. Many of the mounts on the table, particularly the female corner mounts and the paw feet, are found on pieces of furniture that are attributed to André-Charles Boulle and his sons.

Chairs, corners of tables, and inkstands are often seen in French portraits of this period. This table, or its twin, can be seen almost in its entirety in a portrait of Said Pasha, the ambassador of the Sublime Porte (Constantinople), painted by J.-A.-J. Aved (1702-1766) in 1742. It now hangs at Versailles.

On the interior carcase of the table is a drawing in pencil and chalk for a gilt bronze corner mount. It is quite small and not very easy to read, but it is an interesting document of a cabinetmaker's sudden inspiration, using the wood to hand in his workshop rather than a piece of paper.

French (Paris); c. 1725

Height: 2' 5" (73.7 cm.)

Width: 6' 7" (200.7 cm.)

Depth: 2' 11" (89 cm.)

Accession number 67.DA.10

Veneered with amaranth and tulipwood with gilt bronze mounts.

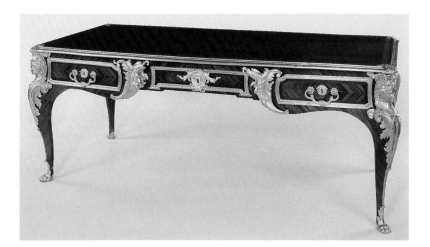

The tureens and stands are variously marked with the date letters for 1726 and 1728, with the charge and discharge marks for the *fermier-généraux* Charles Cordier (1722–1726) and Jacques Cottin (1726–1732) and with their weights. Each stand bears three obliterated marks, and their under-surfaces are inscribed, FAIT PAR F. T. GERMAIN ORF. SCULP. DU ROY AUX GALLERIES DU LOUVRE A PARIS — one with the added date 1764. In spite of this inscription, the tureens and their stands are given to Thomas Germain (b. 1673, master 1720, d. 1748), the father of François-Thomas Germain.

A pair of lidded tureens of the same model but with different stands, stamped with the mark of Thomas Germain, is divided between American and French private collections. The museum's tureens are date-marked for 1726 and 1728, years when the son, François-Thomas (p. 50), was a child. It is likely that the son obtained his father's tureens from an as yet unknown source and, in order to fulfill a commission, obliterated his father's marks, inscribed the platters with his own name, and sold them in 1764 to Melo e Castro, the Portuguese ambassador to Paris, whose arms they bear.

Thomas Germain was the most eminent silversmith of the first half of the eighteenth century. He was trained by the painter Louis Boullogne and was sent to the French Academy in Rome under the protection of Minister Louvois in 1685. He then apprenticed himself to an Italian smith and worked for Cosimo III, the Grand Duke of Tuscany. Returning to Paris in 1706, he became in 1723 *orfèvre du roi* and was granted lodgings in the Louvre. He worked not only for the royal house of France but also for the crowned heads of Portugal, Brazil, Spain, and Naples. At his death the comte de Caylus wrote his eulogy, and John V of Portugal celebrated a funeral service in his memory in Lisbon.

Tureens similar to the museum's are shown filled with fruit in two still life paintings by Alexandre-François Desportes. One painting, in the Nationalmuseum in Stockholm, shows a single tureen with a stand of the same model as that in this museum; the other, in a French private collection, shows a single tureen with no stand.

It is unlikely that the museum's tureens originally possessed lids, for the design of the liners, incorporating half of the boar's head, would make this impossible. The tureens and their stands are extremely heavy, and, as with other French silver of this elaboration and weight, it is unlikely that they were much used. They were probably intended mainly for display amongst other such pieces on a sideboard in the dining room.

French (Paris); 1726–1728

Tureen 1
Height: 6¾" (17.2 cm.)
Width: 1' 6⅜" (46.7 cm.)
Depth: 10⅜" (26.3 cm.)

Tureen 2
Height: 6⅞" (17.4 cm.)
Width: 1' 6½" (47 cm.)
Depth: 10" (25.4 cm.)

Stand 1
Height: 1⅜" (3.5 cm.)
Width: 1' 10⁵⁄₁₆" (56.7 cm.)
Depth: 1' 4" (40.6 cm.)

Stand 2
Height: 1⁷⁄₁₆" (3.7 cm.)
Width: 1' 10⁷⁄₁₆" (57 cm.)
Depth: 1' 4" (40.6 cm.)

Accession number
82.DG.12.1-2

Silver.

The large rooms of the Parisian *hôtels* were notoriously drafty, particularly as the rooms led one into another *en filade* without the protective architectural feature of a corridor. Screens of many forms were employed to protect the inhabitants from heat, light, and drafts. Small fire screens were called *écrans*, and large folding screens such as the one illustrated were known as *paravents* (literally, "against the wind").

Paravents were made with as many as six panels, and it is thought that some originally had decorative surfaces on both the back and the front. The panels on the museum's screen are of knotted wools, exactly like a carpet. They were produced at the Savonnerie manufactory, as was the carpet shown in No. 1. The cartoons for the panels were painted by the animal painter Alexandre-François Desportes (1661-1743) and though these particular designs were knotted throughout the century, the borders were changed from time to time to suit the prevailing fashion. Panels such as those found on the museum's screen were produced in 1735, 1768, and 1772. Judging from the borders of this screen, it would have been made in the earlier period.

A number of Savonnerie *paravents* survive, both in museums and in private collections. One of the finest is in the Musée du Louvre; it includes a panel showing leopards eating grapes. The painted cartoon by Desportes for this is in the Metropolitan Museum of Art, New York. Many of these screens are now rather faded, the dye used for textiles being particularly susceptible to light. The colors of the museum's screen are still strong, but they too are faded in comparison with the wool color samples from Savonnerie that still exist. These samples have always been kept in boxes, and their range and strength of color is very startling.

French (Savonnerie); c. 1735

Height: 5' 11½" (181.6 cm.)
Width: 8' (243.8 cm.)

Accession number 75.DH.1

Knotted wool, linen warp and weft. The wooden interior frame and the velvet backing are modern.

This unusual wall clock has a case completely made of Chantilly porcelain. The porcelain manufactory of Chantilly was owned by the Prince de Condé, who was following the then pervasive desire of a number of princes, kings, and emperors to establish their own porcelain works. The factory began to produce in 1725 under the inspired leadership of Ciquaire Cirou. The early products were, in the main, copies of Japanese porcelain, of which the Prince had a large collection. Unlike other contemporary factories, Chantilly used the opaque tin glaze rather than the more translucent lead glaze. This clock case dates to about 1740, and by this date the factory was producing objects in the contemporary native style. The remains of an oriental influence can be seen in the incorporation of an exotic dragon and a monkey into the design.

The face and the movement of the clock are inscribed CHARLES VOISIN APARIS. Voisin became a master in 1710 and died in 1760. One of the main wheels of the movement is covered with inscriptions placed there, as was the custom, by various clock repairers. Most are indecipherable, but the dates 1756, 1768, 1817, and 1854 can be read.

The clock, of a type sometimes known as a *pendule d'alcove*, was perhaps intended to be hung in a bed alcove. It strikes to the nearest hour when a string, protruding from the movement through the porcelain case, is pulled — a useful device to learn the time in the dark without having to light a candle.

One other wall clock with a case of Chantilly porcelain exists in the Metropolitan Museum of Art, New York. It is a little smaller in size, and the case is decorated with Chinese figures.

French (Chantilly): c. 1740

Height: 2' 5½" (74.9 cm.)
Width: 1' 2" (35.6 cm.)
Depth: 4⅜" (11.1 cm.)

Accession number 81.DB.81

Soft paste porcelain and gilt bronze, with an enamel dial.

This commode is fitted with two doors and was known as a *commode à vantaux*. The shaped oval cartouche in the center of the front, outlined by an attenuated and scrolling gilt bronze mount, is set with Japanese lacquer taken from the doors of a cabinet. The rest of the surface is painted in imitation of lacquer in a technique known as *Vernis Martin*, after the Martin brothers who invented the most successful and widely used imitation lacquer in the mid–eighteenth century.

Throughout the late seventeenth and eighteenth centuries there was an interest in France, indeed a passion, for oriental objects. The opening up of trade with the East through ventures such as the Dutch East India Company encouraged the vogue for such objects, as did the visits of the Siamese "embassies" to Louis XIV in 1684 and 1686. This fashion swiftly led to the production of objects in the Chinese style, termed "chinoiserie." On this commode we see a combination of oriental lacquer and a French imitation of it. Japanese lacquer was scarce, and inventive lacquerers such as the Martin brothers were soon able to produce rather convincing copies of it. Unfortunately the French imitation is extremely fragile and, painted directly onto the carcase wood, it has usually suffered with the passage of time.

In 1751 the guild of *menuisiers-ébénistes* required all cabinet and chair makers to stamp their works with their name. This commode is stamped on the surface of the wood beneath the marble top, BVRB. It was not until the 1950's that these initials were understood to stand for Bernard van Risenburgh, perhaps the most innovative and skilled cabinetmaker of the mid–eighteenth century. This commode is very typical of his work; and framing and corner mounts of the same model are found on a number of his commodes nearly all of which are decorated with lacquer.

In 1737 van Risenburgh delivered, through the *marchand-mercier* (see p. 46) Hébert, a similarly mounted lacquer commode to Maria Leczinska, Louis XV's Queen, for her use in the *Cabinet de la Reine* at the Château de Fontainebleau; it is now in a French private collection. That delivery date enables us to date this commode quite precisely.

French (Paris); c. 1735–1740

Height: 2′ 11″ (88.8 cm.)
Width: 4′ 11¾″ (151.9 cm.)
Depth: 1′ 9½″ (54.6 cm.)

Accession number 65.DA.4

Painted with *Vernis Martin,* set with a panel of Japanese lacquer, with gilt bronze mounts.

The marble top dates to about 1600 and was probably made in Rome, rather than in the Medici workshops in Florence. The Florentine workshops, which still exist as the *Museo dell' Opificio delle pietre dure*, were set up in 1580 and have produced works in *pietre dure* or hard stones up until this day. The Florentine practice was to set the pieces of stone into a veneer of slate, which was then attached to a marble base. In Rome, the colored stones were set directly into the white matrix of marble (the *comesso* technique), and veneerings of slate were only rarely used. As this table top shows a combination of both techniques, it is more likely to have been made in Rome.

When the Manufacture Royale de la Couronne at the Gobelins was set up by Colbert, a number of Italian workers in *pietre dure* were brought from Italy to make plaques for the furniture destined for Louis XIV's residences. The craft was soon learned by native French craftsmen, and the hardstone plaques used for this kind of decoration were extremely popular in France.

Italian works in this technique were avidly acquired by young noblemen, particularly the English, on the Grand Tour; and it is possible that this table top was acquired by a young Frenchman during his travels in the mid-eighteenth century. A few table tops of this size and complexity still exist at Charlecote (bought by William Beckford from the Palazzo Borghese), at Powis Castle in Wales, and at the Metropolitan Museum of Art in New York. All three have nineteenth- or twentieth-century bases.

The base of the museum's table, though of carved oak, is not really strong enough to support the extremely heavy top; and it is surprising that it has survived. It is similar in design to a table shown in a portrait of Maria Leczinska which was exhibited in the *salon* of 1747 by Carle van Loo (now in the Musée du Louvre). Both tables have legs of similar profile, with large scallop shells above and incurling feet, and with the frieze carved with garlands of flowers. The museum's table is more elaborate, with winged serpents twined around the leafy stretchers. An oriental porcelain vase would probably have been placed on the plinth at the center. As with almost all carved tables of this date, the name of the maker is not known.

The marble top: Italian (Roman); c. 1600
The base: French (Paris); c. 1745

Height: 2′ 10½″ (87.7 cm.)
Width: 6′ 6″ (198.1 cm.)
Depth: 3′ 9½″ (115.6 cm.)

Accession number 72.DA.58

Gilded oak, the top of white marble veneered with slate, set with lapis lazuli, verde antique, oriental alabaster, chalcedony, rosso antico, nero antico, agate, jasper, carnelian, and other semiprecious stones.

These elaborate assemblages consist of separate elements of Chinese porcelain put together with gilt bronze mounts by a Parisian *fondeur-doreur*. They were made during the years marking the height of the fashion for mounting oriental porcelain but are of a more unusual and elaborate form than the simpler gilt bronze mounted vessels.

The porcelain boys personify the spirit of accord, known as the "Twin Immortals of Harmony" (Hehe Erxian). They were the patron deities of Chinese merchants in general and of Chinese potters in particular. The pierced globes may in China have held perfume balls and in their French form may have held potpourri. But with such fanciful objects, it is not always possible to designate a specific use, and they were perhaps intended to be purely decorative.

There are numerous examples of mounted oriental porcelain that have small lizards and shells on their bases. They were probably all made in the same workshop, but it is likely that we shall never know the name of this inventive craftsman.

The survival of such fragile composite objects is rare, and few are known today. There are some repaired breaks here and there, but the necks and tails of the birds and the leaves and petals of the plants climbing the rockwork bases have remained intact.

The porcelain:
Chinese, Kangxi, c. 1700
and Qianlong; c. 1740.
The mounts:
French (Paris); c. 1745.

Height: 11¾" (29.9 cm.)
Width: 8⅞" (22.5 cm.)
Depth: 5¼" (13.2 cm.)

Accession number
78.DI.4.1–2

Porcelain with gilt bronze mounts.

33

Fire dogs, or *chenets*, were placed in the hearth of a fireplace. They were used to support the fire-tongs and poker (*pelles* and *pincettes*) and had iron attachments at the back for this purpose, which have usually since been removed. Simpler fire dogs, usually of brass with larger iron extensions, were used to support the logs and coals.

These fire dogs are in the high rococo style and exhibit a certain fancifulness typical of the period. The lounging females are half-human and half-animal, with large hairy legs and paws; paws also replace their hands. One holds a cat and the other, a monkey. They were made by Charles Cressent (1685-1768), the great *bronzier* and cabinetmaker who was patronized by the duc d'Orléans. He was trained as a sculptor in the Académie de Saint Luc, and, contrary to the strict guild regulations of Paris, he had a forge and gilders in his workshop. He designed and produced his own gilt bronzes — fire dogs such as these, clocks, and mounts for his furniture. This craft was supposed to be carried out only by the guild of *fondeurs-doreurs*. Cressent's workshop was regularly investigated by the guild, and he was often fined for this infringement. In order to pay these fines, he held sales of his stock and wrote the catalogues himself. In such a sale catalogue, written in 1756 (for a sale which did not eventually take place), we find the following lot:

> *No. 163 - Dans son salon à la cheminée, un feu qui représente deux Sphinx, dont un badine avec un chat et l'autre avec un singe, montés sur deux pieds, du plus grand goût. Les amateurs remarqueront que ces sphinx ne sont pas traités comme ceux qui se font ordinairement pour des feux, ceux-ci peuvent être considérés comme ce qu'il y a de mieux traité en France, garni des ses agraffes dorées d'or moulu.*

Other models of these fire dogs exist in private collections. They have sometimes been regilded, but the museum's examples retain their original gilding, worn very slightly here and there.

French (Paris); c. 1745-1750

Height: 1' 3¼" (38.7 cm.)
Width: 1' 3" (38.1 cm.)
Depth: 8" (20.3 cm.)

Accession number
73.DF.63.1-2.

Gilded bronze.

It is unfortunate that the movement for this highly complex terrestrial and celestial clock is missing. The dials show us that the clock originally gave the time simultaneously in Paris and in different cities and countries around the globe, such as "*Guatamale-Floride*", "*La Californie*", "*Jendo au Japon*", and "*Samarcande en Gde Tartarie*". It also indicated the day of the week, the day of the month, the month, the zodiacal sign, the times of the tides in French and English ports, the phase of the moon, and the time of the eclipse of the first moon of Jupiter, Io. The small central dial is inscribed "*Inventé par A. Fortier*". Alexandre Fortier's dates are not known, but he was a mathematician and inventor as well as a *Notaire de Paris*, working in the first half of the eighteenth century. Two working planispheres complete with their cases are known. One is in the Wallace Collection, London. It was made for Paris de Montmartel in the early 1760's, with a movement by Stollewerck and Fortier. The other, in a French private collection, is dated 1765 and also has a movement by these two men.

In the Conservatoire des Arts et des Métiers, Paris, there are a number of planisphere movements or parts of movements. One of the earlier ones, by Mathieu Kriegseissen, is dated 1726. It is inscribed with exactly the same cities and countries as the museum's planisphere, in the same order, with the same misspellings. It is possible that the information provided on these clocks was taken from the same source book.

The case itself, with its distinctive form and florid mounts, is attributed to Jean-Pierre Latz (c. 1791-1754) (see No. 24). All the mounts on the lower section, which would have housed the weights, are marked with the crowned C tax stamp (see p. 38), but none of the mounts on the upper section are so marked. This indicates that the upper section may have been made before 1745 and the lower part completed after this date.

A very similar planisphere is described in the 1777 sale catalogue of the Prince de Conti, who lived in the Hôtel du Temple in considerable luxury. Such powerful and cultivated men were interested not only in the arts but also in science and technology. This clock shows both aspects of such interests, which were fostered and developed at a time which is now known as the Age of Enlightenment.

French (Paris); c. 1745-1750

Height: 9′ 3″ (281.9 cm.)
Width: 3′ 1″ (93.5 cm.)
Depth: 1′ 3″ (38.1 cm.)

Accession number 74.DB.2

Veneered with kingwood and tulipwood, with gilt bronze mounts and brass dials.

This commode can be dated to between the years 1745 and 1749 because of the presence of a tax stamp that has been struck on the gilt bronze corner mounts. This stamp takes the form of a very small C surmounted by a crown. It was struck to show that a tax had been paid on the copper (*cuivre*) content of the bronze mount, and the tax was only levied in these four years.

The commode, purely in the régence style, is rather old-fashioned for this date when the rococo style was already at its height. It was made by Charles Cressent (1685-1768); and all of the mounts, with the exception of the corner mounts and the central mount on the upper drawer, are found on a number of his commodes. It should be noticed that the marquetry has been designed so that the mounts lie on the darker ground of amaranth, outlined by the lighter tulipwood. The only concession that Cressent has made to the rococo style is to treat the entire front as an area for one continuous design, unbroken by the drawers' fronts and the old-fashioned divider between them.

In the sale catalogue written by Cressent in 1756 (already referred to in the text for No. 17), we find the following entry:

No. 132. Une commode de quatre pieds, marbre Breche violette, les bronzes représentant deux enfans qui rapent du tabac, au milieu est un singe qui se poudre de tabac, dorés d'or moulu.

That this commode was still in his possession some ten years after its construction indicates that it did not sell. Indeed, Cressent made no other commode exactly like it, whereas a number of his commodes duplicate each other. It is interesting to note that Mr. Getty bought this commode in 1938 for only $5,000. It was one of the first pieces of French furniture that he acquired.

French (Paris); c. 1745-1749

Height: 2' 11½" (90.2 cm.)
Width: 4' 5¾" (136.5 cm.)
Depth: 2' 1½" (64.8 cm.)

Accession number
70.DA.82

Veneered with tulipwood and amaranth, with gilt bronze mounts.

The commodes are both stamped BVRB and were made by Bernard van Risenburgh. They are not typical of his work, and this may be because they were not made for a French client. The work of the Parisian cabinetmakers was much in demand in Germany, Russia, and even Poland; and it is often seen that the subtle French style was made more exuberant and flamboyant to suit the taste of these farther-flung societies of different cultures.

According to tradition these commodes, part of a set with three larger commodes and a pair of corner cupboards, were made for the Elector of Saxony, Frederick Augustus II, the father-in-law of Louis, the Grand Dauphin. They are listed in a 1794 inventory of the Elector's household and were, at least by the early twentieth century, in the Zimmer König Augustus III at Schloss Moritzburg, the residence of the former royal house of Wettin.

From the decoration of the set of furniture, it is likely that they were always intended for a hunting lodge such as Moritzburg. On the fronts of the commodes are stags at bay, and the corner mounts are overlaid with hunting trophies. The mount showing a stag at bay may have been inspired by an engraving after Jean-Baptiste Oudry's *Le Chevreuil Forcé*. The corner cupboards, unfortunately destroyed in the Second World War, were similarly decorated. The three large commodes, which are heavily mounted with stags and boars, are now in the Schloss Pillnitz, near Dresden. The museum's two commodes were acquired by Anna Thompson Dodge in 1934.

Although the massive and unrestricted design of the mounts is not found elsewhere in van Risenburgh's oeuvre, it should be remembered that he was an extremely versatile cabinetmaker. He made use of both lacquer and marquetry and was probably the first cabinetmaker to use Sèvres porcelain plaques to decorate his furniture. He was also an inventor of forms, as is shown by the double desk in No. 22.

French (Paris); c. 1750

Height: 2' 10⅜" (87.3 cm.)
Width: 3' 4⅛" (101.9 cm.)
Depth: 1' 10" (55.8 cm.)

Accession number
71.DA.96.1-2

Veneered with tulipwood, kingwood, and amaranth, with gilt bronze mounts.

This large corner cabinet is stamped I. DUBOIS in several places for Jacques Dubois (b. c. 1693, master 1742, d. 1763). The work of Dubois, usually in the rococo style, was always of high quality. The face and the movement of the clock are inscribed "Etienne le Noir" (b. 1724, master 1743, d. after 1791), a leading Parisian clockmaker of the period.

The form and decoration of this cabinet are unique, although simple corner cupboards of more usual, small size do exist with a range of shelves above them. The design of this piece closely follows a drawing by Nicolas Pineau (1684–1755), which was engraved by Jean Mariette, probably in the 1730's The engraving shows the corner cabinet, topped by shelves and a clock, with candelabra held by babies sitting on lions, in a rather plain interior with a bed in an alcove. The paneling and the bed are in the régence style.

The exuberance of the cabinet does not conform to the taste of Parisian society, and, indeed, it was made for Count Jan Klemens Branicki, the Grand Hetman of the Crown of Poland. It appears in a posthumous inventory, written in 1772, of the contents of his palace in Warsaw. In the grand salon stood, "A Paris corner cupboard with two candelabra each in gilt metal and on top a Paris clock...". The inventory goes on to describe the objects displayed on the shelves: a collection of mounted Chinese porcelain, some with clocks, and all embellished with porcelain flowers.

The count was buying French furniture and objects in Paris in the 1750's. The drawing by Pineau, or the engraving of it, must have come to his attention. It seems that Dubois was commissioned, probably by a Monsieur Lullier, a Warsaw *marchand-mercier*, to construct the cabinet for the Polish aristocrat. The Szymanowski family inherited the cabinet. The Szymanowskis probably sold it to the Viennese branch of the Rothschild family, who in turn sold it to the famous family of art dealers, the Wildensteins.

In the mid-eighteenth century the ties between the Polish and French courts were close, and Branicki's third wife was related to the King of Poland, whose daughter was Louis XV's Queen. It seems that the full-blown rococo style was popular with Polish society. In 1734 Juste-Aurèle Meissonier delivered to Count Bielinski a *cabinet* complete with paneling, ceiling, and marble mantelpiece, which he installed in his palace outside Warsaw. Perhaps the most unrestrained of all rococo interiors, the Meissonier room is known today only from engravings and drawings. It is highly likely that Branicki would have known Bielinski and his *cabinet*, and it may well have influenced his taste.

French (Paris); c. 1750

Height: 9' 6" (289.5 cm.)
Width: 4' 3" (129.5 cm.)
Depth: 2' 4½" (72 cm.)

Accession number
79.DA.66

Veneered with tulipwood and kingwood, with gilt bronze mounts.

The double form of this desk is unique. On both sides there are writing surfaces which can be lowered to reveal drawers and pigeon holes. The desk is stamped BVRB for Bernard van Risenburgh (master before 1730, d. 1765/66), who was also the maker of the lacquer commode shown as No. 14. This desk, in his later style, is much more massive; but the quality of every detail is of the highest order. The mounts are finely cast and chased, and the trailing foliage marquetry of the end-cut kingwood is carefully arranged to fill the areas designated in a graceful, uncluttered way. Even the interior hinges to the writing surfaces are held by large engraved gilt bronze plates.

It is not known for whom the desk was made, though it has been suggested that it was made for the use of the twin daughters — Sophie and Adelaide — of Louis XV. But if this were true, the desk would be listed in one of the royal inventories and would certainly bear some sort of inventory number or château mark. We do know that the desk was bought in Paris in the 1760's by Elizabeth Gunning, one of the great beauties of the court of George II, who had married John, 5th Duke of Argyll, in 1759. The desk remained in the Argyll family until it was sold by the 11th Duke in the early 1950's.

A similar desk, but not of double form, also made by Bernard van Risenburgh, is in the collection of the Earl of Rosebery at Dalmeny House, Scotland.

French (Paris); c. 1750

Height: 3' 6½" (107.8 cm.)
Width: 5' 2½" (158.7 cm.)
Depth: 2' 9⅜" (84.7 cm.)

Accession number
70.DA.87

Veneered with tulipwood and kingwood, with gilt bronze mounts.

The front of this commode is set with three panels of Japanese lacquer, the seams of which are hidden by the meandering gilt bronze framing mounts. The remaining areas of the commode are lacquered with imitation *nashiji*. The mounts are of the highest quality, and the edge of the marble top is carved below its rim, a most unusual refinement. It is all of the quality that one would expect from the cabinetmaker Joseph Baumhauer; and although he has not stamped this piece, it can be firmly attributed to him. A number of commodes of the same model exist, decorated with lacquer or marquetry, and most of them are stamped JOSEPH. The date of Baumhauer's mastership has been given by earlier furniture historians as 1765; but this must be incorrect, as he died after a long illness in 1772 and could not possibly have produced the many pieces stamped by him in the space of some five years. The majority of his works are, like the commode, in the rococo style; and he probably became a master in the early 1740's.

Glued to the carcase beneath the marble top and also to the underside of the commode are the printed trade labels of Charles Darnault. Darnault was a member of the guild of *marchands-mercier*. These men were elegant shopkeepers who sold furniture, porcelains, gold boxes, mounted porcelains and expensive trinkets to the members of the Court and Parisian society. Cabinetmakers such as Joseph Baumhauer and Bernard van Risenburgh seem to have been commissioned directly by the *marchands-mercier*, and it was the *marchands-mercier* who probably invented the ideas of mounting furniture with lacquer and Sèvres porcelain plaques and of setting oriental porcelain with gilt bronze mounts. They were the inventors and purveyors of fashion and played an extremely important role in supplying a rich and novelty-seeking society with expensive furniture and trinkets in the new styles for its homes. Darnault, whose shop called *Au Roy d'Espagne* was on the rue de la Monnaie, near the Pont Neuf, declared on his trade label that he sold the following: mirrors, wall lights, inkstands, chandeliers, clocks, marble topped tables, painted overdoors, toilette sets, cabinets, screens, writing desks, secrétaires, armoires, bookcases, "*et toutes sortes d'autres choses pour meubler les Appartements*." Many of these items are described as "*vernis de la Chine & du Japon*."

French (Paris); c. 1750

Height: 2' 10¾" (88.3 cm.)
Width: 4' 9½" (146.1 cm.)
Depth: 2' ⅝" (62.6 cm.)

Accession number 55.DA.2

Set with panels of Japanese lacquer, with gilt bronze mounts.

These four corner cupboards do not, strictly speaking, form a set, as one pair is slightly taller than the other. Otherwise they are of the same shape and design, with identical mounts. They do not bear the stamp of a cabinetmaker but are attributed to Jean-Pierre Latz (b. c. 1691, d. 1754), a cabinetmaker whose work, with its slight heaviness of design and distinctive mounts, is fairly easy to recognize. Latz, like Charles Cressent (see No. 17), defied the rules of the guilds by modeling and casting his own bronze mounts. For this infringement, he, like Cressent, was fined a number of times. Inventories were made of the offending mounts in his workshops, and these descriptions help us to identify his works. A number of the mounts on these corner cupboards are also found on pieces of furniture stamped by him or on pieces of furniture which bear these and other mounts, which in their turn appear on stamped pieces. For this reason the attribution must remain a little tentative.

However, there is no doubt about the name of the maker of the extremely fine panels of floral marquetry. It is surely Jean-François Oeben, who was appointed royal cabinetmaker in 1754 and was the master of the equally famous royal cabinetmaker of the later decades of the eighteenth century, Jean-Henri Riesener (p. 82). Nearly all of the individual flowers on the cabinet doors can be found on pieces stamped with Oeben's name; and they are very typical of his work, with their subtle shading achieved by scorching with hot sand, their dark leaves, and the lifelike way in which the flower stems are cut. The lilies seen on the right-hand door of the cabinet are taken from an engraving by Louis Tessier (c. 1719-1781), and they are often found on Oeben's work. There are no records to show any association between Latz and Oeben, though it is known that specialists in marquetry, such as Oeben, sometimes worked as *marqueteurs* for other cabinetmakers. It is possible that Oeben acquired the unfinished carcases after the death of Latz, but for a major cabinetmaker of the stature of Oeben to do so seems a little unlikely.

French (Paris); c. 1750-1755

Illustrated:
Height: 3' 2" (96.5 cm.)
Width: 2' 10" (86.4 cm.)
Depth: 1' 11¾" (59 cm.)

Not illustrated:
Height: 2' 11½" (90.2 cm.)
Width: 2' 7" (78.7 cm.)
Depth: 1' 11" (58.4 cm.)

Accession numbers
72.DA.39.1-2; 72.DA.69.1-2

Veneered with amaranth, satinwood, and a marquetry of natural and stained exotic and fruit woods, with gilt bronze mounts.

49

These wall lights, in the form of bunches of laurel tied with a ribbon, were made in 1756 by François-Thomas Germain (b. 1726, master 1748, d. 1791), the celebrated *orfèvre du roi*, who is better known for his works in silver. The lights are of massive size; but in their casting, chasing, and burnishing, they have been handled with all the attention given to detail found on one of Germain's pieces of silver.

Each wall light is cast from a different model, and the pairs do not repeat each other. Two are inscribed FAIT PAR F. T. GERMAIN SCULP^T.ORFR^E. DU ROY. AUX GALLERIES DU LOUVRE A PARIS 1756. They were made for the duc d'Orléans and were hung at the Palais Royal, two in his *Chambre de Parade* and two in the *Salle des Jeux*. They may have been designed by the architect Contant d'Ivry, who was redecorating the interiors of the palace at this time. They are shown *in situ* in two engravings of the rooms in Diderot and d'Alembert's *Encyclopédie, ou Dictionnaire Raisonné des Sciences*...in the volume of plates printed in 1762.

At the private sale of the duc d'Orléans' possessions in 1783, the wall lights were bought by the Crown; and they were hung in the *Salon des Nobles de la Reine* at the Château de Compiègne. All four lights are numbered 28 and bear a crowned CP, the château mark for Compiègne. During the Revolution, the wall lights were not sold but were reserved by the *commission de commerce*. They were hung in the Palais du Luxembourg, and each was stamped LUX 1051. At some point in the latter part of the nineteenth century, they were acquired by Baron Mayer de Rothschild and hung at Mentmore Towers. They passed by descent to the Earls of Rosebery.

The design of the wall lights is unique, and very few pieces of gilt bronze are so well documented. Only two other signed works of gilt bronze by Germain are known, a pair of fire dogs in the Musée du Louvre and the mounts of a mantelpiece in Bernstorff Castle, Copenhagen.

French (Paris); 1756

1. Height: 3' 3¼" (99.6 cm.)
Width: 2' ⅞" (63.2 cm.)
Depth: 1' 4⅛" (41 cm.)
2. Height: 3' 1¼" (94.6 cm.)
Width: 1' 11⅝" (57.5 cm.)
Depth: 1' 1⅝" (34.6 cm.)
3. Height: 3' 4½" (102.9 cm.)
Width: 2' 1" (63.5 cm.)
Depth: 1' 1½" (34.3 cm.)
4. Height: 2' 11⅛" (89.2 cm.)
Width: 1' 10⅜" (56.8 cm.)
Depth: 1' 3⁷⁄₁₀" (40.3 cm.)

Accession number
81.DF.96.1-4

Gilded bronze.

This soft paste porcelain basket has panels of green ground color highlighted with gilding. It is painted beneath the base with the crossed L's of the Sèvres Manufactory enclosing the date letter D for 1756. The basket is also incised with the mark PZ of the modeler, or *répareur*, who carried out the detailed work of tidying up the modeling of the shape after it had been taken from the mold.

Only one other basket of this model and size is known to have survived. That one is formed with strapwork around the body in a slightly different pattern of chevrons and with differently arranged ribbons at the junctions of the handle and the rim of the basket. It is also decorated with a green ground and has slightly more elaborate gilding over the ground color. There is a larger Sèvres porcelain basket in the Wallace Collection in London, but it does not have the elaboration of the ribbons at each end of the handle.

In the sales registers of the Sèvres Manufactory for December 1757, a basket is mentioned which would appear to have been one of the museum's model. A "*panier 2ème grandeur, vert*" valued at 240 *livres*, was given to the painter François Boucher. Boucher supplied designs to the porcelain manufactory in the form of drawings, and the designers there also made use of published engravings after his paintings. His work was used as the inspiration both for the many biscuit porcelain figures produced from the 1750's onward and also for the painted scenes on a wide variety of wares through several decades.

The Sèvres porcelain manufactory was begun in the 1740's as a private enterprise aiming to produce this sought-after material in France. The original workshops were housed in the Château de Vincennes. The factory moved to Sèvres in 1756 after Louis XV had become the major shareholder in the company, probably as a result of the encouragement of Madame de Pompadour. The King's mistress was a keen purchaser of Vincennes and Sèvres products. As the Royal Porcelain Manufactory, the Sèvres kilns produced some of the most lavishly decorated wares of the eighteenth century in Europe. A monopoly was granted to Sèvres to produce gilded porcelains, and the manufactory's products ranged from simple domestic wares, such as cups and saucers, to elaborate dinner services and *garnitures* of ornamental vases, richly decorated with ground colors, painted scenes, and gilding.

French (Sèvres); 1756

Height: 8' ¾" (22.0 cm.)
Width: 7' ⅞" (20.1 cm.)
Diameter: 7" (18.0 cm.)

Accession number
82.DE.92

Soft paste porcelain.

This small table is stamped J.F. OEBEN for the royal cabinet-maker Jean-François Oeben (b. c. 1720, royal cabinetmaker 1754, master 1761, d. 1763). It displays two of the characteristics for which he is so well known: fine marquetry and complicated fittings. The top of the table slides back. A drawer which occupies the whole of the body of the piece can be pulled out, and the drawer itself has a sliding top, released by depressing a button. The interior is divided into compartments and lined with pale blue silk. The sliding top of the drawer is covered with trellis marquetry with a shaped panel of leather in the center, tooled and gilt with lilies around its edge; the leather itself is stained to resemble burr wood. The sides of the drawer are also veneered with trellis marquetry.

The top of the table has equally elaborate marquetry. In the center is a basket of flowers, surrounded by garlands of other flowers suspended from a trellis and twining through and around interlacing strapwork. At the four corners are a lion, a swan, a dove, and a salamander representing the four elements: Earth, Water, Air, and Fire.

A very similar table appears in a painting of Madame de Pompadour by François Guérin. As she is shown with her daughter, Alexandrine, who died in 1754, it must have been painted before that date. Madame de Pompadour was a patron of Oeben, and the table in the painting could be the museum's table or a closely similar one in the Musée du Louvre.

One of the first objects that Oeben made for the Crown was an invalid chair for the sickly son of the Dauphin, Louis duc de Bourgogne (1751-1761). The chair has disappeared, but it is known to have incorporated elaborate mechanical fittings. The museum possesses a mechanical table by Oeben, which springs open at the turn of a key, its movement activated by a series of springs and ratchets. As he needed a considerable amount of iron for his complicated mechanisms, Oeben's workshop was housed at the Arsenal, whose foundry he could use.

French (Paris); c. 1754

Height: 2′ 4″ (71.1 cm.)
Width: 2′ 7½″ (80 cm.)
Depth: 1′ 4⅞″ (42.8 cm.)

Accession number
71.DA.103

Veneered with tulipwood, kingwood, amaranth, burr wood, and stained and natural exotic woods, with gilt bronze mounts.

These vases are made of soft paste porcelain with enameled decoration and three ground colors — pink, green, and dark blue (*bleu lapis*) — with gilding. One of these vases bears the crossed L's mark of the Sèvres Manufactory. This elaborate model was called a *vase pot pourri à dauphin* or a *vase pot pourri fontaine* in the eighteenth-century documents which are still at Sèvres. The vases were made to hold potpourri in the tall central sections, which are pierced. The lower section was designed to contain small flowering bulbs which could be fed with water through the lozenge-shaped holes. The vases were most probably provided with porcelain flowers on gilt bronze stems to be placed in the bulb holes as an alternative to live flowers. The plaster model for this shape still survives at Sèvres. Only three other vases of this model are known, one in the British Royal Collection and a pair in the collection of the Duke of Buccleuch.

The chinoiserie scenes painted on these vases are attributed to Charles-Nicolas Dodin (active at Sèvres 1754-1803). Approximately a dozen pieces of Sèvres porcelain survive that are decorated with this type of oriental scene; all of them date from between 1760 and 1763, and some are marked by Dodin.

These vases are known as the Dudley Vases after one of their former owners, William Humble, 1st Earl of Dudley. They were in the Dudley Collection from 1874 to the 1920's. However, the first record of them is in the *Régistres des Ventes de la Manufacture de Vincennes et Sèvres* of May 30, 1760, when they were sold for 960 *livres* in cash. The next mention of these vases is found in the inventory taken after the death of Madame de Pompadour in 1764. They are listed in her *chambre du lit* of the Hôtel Pompadour in Paris, now the Palais de l'Elysée. They are described together with a *vase vaisseau à mât*, two *vases à bobèches*, and two porcelain wall lights of matching decoration forming a *garniture de cheminée*. The whereabouts of the two *vases à bobèches*, is not known, but the *vaisseau* (of the same form as the Getty *vaisseau* in No. 29) and the wall lights are in a French private collection. The museum's vases also passed through the collections of the Duchess of Cleveland, William Goding, the Earl of Coventry, and, as mentioned above, the Earl of Dudley, who also at one time owned the museum's *vaisseau à mât*.

French (Sèvres); c. 1760
Height: 11¾" (29.8 cm.)
Width: 6½" (16.5 cm.)
Depth: 5¾" (14.6 cm.)
Accession number
78.DE.358.1-2
Soft paste porcelain.

This boat-shaped vase is made of soft paste porcelain. It has a pierced lid in the form of rigging so that the scent of the pot-pourri it contained could mix with the air in the room. The vase is decorated with pink and green ground colors and bears a date letter and a painter's mark that are no longer legible. The front panel has a reserve painted with a Teniers-like scene of a woman scolding a drunken man, attributed to the painter Charles-Nicolas Dodin (active at Sèvres 1754–1803). The other side of the vase has a reserve painted with a bunch of flowers.

This celebrated model was known as a *vase vaisseau à mât*. Although twelve of these vases were certainly produced, only ten have survived into the twentieth century. They all have varying decoration and were made to be sold with other vases of different shapes forming *garnitures*. The boat shape was probably a reference to the single-masted ship found on the coat of arms of the city of Paris. The final model was derived from a series of Sèvres boat-shaped *jardinières* and sauce-boats. The first of these was called a *cuvette à masques* and was designed in 1754, probably by the sculptor Jean-Claude Duplessis. He was active at Sèvres as a designer from 1745 and was head of the modeling studio from that date until 1774.

All of these ten *vases vaisseaux à mât* have pennants on their "masts" decorated with the French royal emblem, the fleur-de-lys, in gold. This would indicate that they were all made for members of the royal family, or as royal gifts. In the eighteenth century, *vaisseaux à mâts* are known to have belonged to the Prince de Condé, to the marquis de Marigny, and to his sister Madame de Pompadour. She owned at least two *vaisseaux*, one of which formed a *garniture* with the two *vases pot pourri fontaine* in No. 28, together with a pair of *vases à bobèches*, now lost.

French (Sèvres); 1759

Height: 1′ 3″ (38.1 cm.)
Width: 1′ 1¾″ (35 cm.)
Depth: 6¾″ (17.2 cm.)

Accession number 75.DE.11

Soft paste porcelain.

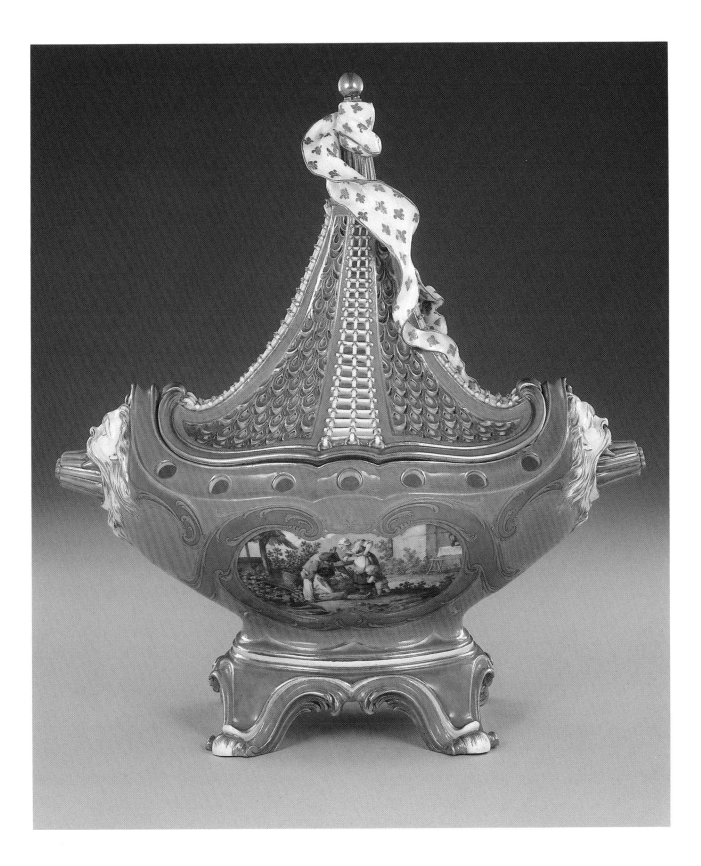

Because of a large inventory number painted on the back of this commode, No. 2556, we are able to identify the maker, its date, and the person for whom it was made. Objects made for members of the French royal family and household were, on delivery, assigned inventory numbers. Details concerning each piece were entered in the *Journal de la Garde Meuble de la Couronne*, which still exists in the French archives. Under No. 2556 we read the following:

du 28 aoust 1769

Livré par le Sr. Joubert
Pour servir dans la Chambre à Coucher de Madame Louise de France au Château de Versailles.

No. 2556.   Deux commodes à la Régence de bois violet et rose à placages en mozaique, ayant par devant deux grand tiroirs fermant par une seule clef et sur les cotez deux armoires fermant à clef avec une tablette en dedans, les panneaux ornez en plein de petites rozettes, les cotés de deux bustes de femmes couronnés de laurier, porté sur deux gaines en mozaique et les corps d'entrées de serrures, boutons, carderons, chutes, rozettes, souspentes, et pieds ferrez par des griffes de lion, le tout en bronze cizelé et surdoré d'or moulu très riches avec leur dessus de marbre dont un griotte d'Italie et l'autre Dantin, longues de 5 pieds et demi sur 24 pouces de profondeur et 34 pouces de hauteur.

The whereabouts of the pair to this commode is unknown. Madame Louise was the eighth daughter of Louis XV, born in 1737 (see No. 33).

Gilles Joubert (b. 1689, royal cabinetmaker 1763-1774, d. 1775) became the royal cabinetmaker after the death of Jean-François Oeben and was replaced in turn by Jean-Henri Riesener in 1774. He was already eighty years old when this commode was made, so it would only have been made under his supervision. Most of Joubert's known works are in the rococo style, and this venture into the neoclassical style has produced a rather ungainly piece. It is, however, as with all royal furniture, beautifully made, the bronze mounts heavily gilded and the marble top of unusual thickness.

French (Paris); 1769
Height: 3′ ½″ (92.7 cm.)
Width: 5′ 11″ (180.3 cm.)
Depth: 2′ 3″ (68.6 cm.)

Accession number 55.DA.5

Veneered with tulipwood, box, and ebony with gilt bronze mounts.

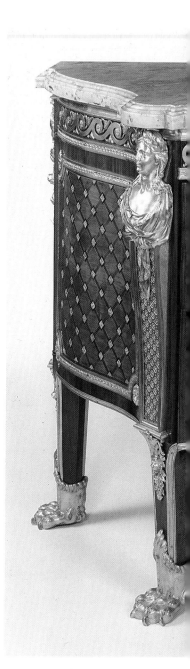

Each corner cupboard is stamped P. GARNIER for Pierre Garnier (b. 1726, master 1742, d. 1800). Garnier had the distinction of working for the marquis de Marigny (1727-1781), the brother of Madame de Pompadour. He provided furniture for the marquis' *hôtel* in the Place des Victoires and for the Château de Menars. Letters from Marigny to Garnier have survived, and they show that Garnier designed much of his own furniture and mounts. Both he and Marigny were fond of the use of ebony, and it is quite possible that these cupboards were made for the marquis, who would have enjoyed their unique form, solidly composed in the newly emergent neoclassical style of which the marquis was such a champion.

In 1779 Marigny was writing to Garnier about a pair of cabinets on which he intended to place heavy bronze sculpture "...*comme je ne me soucie point d'ouvrir ces bas d'armoire vous les construirez intérieurement comme bon vous semblera.*" These could be the corner cupboards under discussion, except that their design indicates a date earlier than 1779. The cupboards take the form of tapering pedestals applied to rectangles, and an engraving for a similar object appears in Diderot's *Encyclopédie* in the volume of plates published in 1765, which supports a date in this earlier period. They are very shallow, being little over a foot in depth, with room for only a small bust or a narrow decorative vase.

The corner cupboards appear in the sale catalogue of a Monsieur Godefroy, 15 November 1785:

> *238bis. Deux Encoignures très-riches, en forme de gaine à fond d'ébene, ornés de guirlandes, rosasses & frises de bronze doré; le reste du devant est en plaquage de palissandre. Elles sont couvertes de leur marbre blanc, de 2 pouces d'épaisseur. Hauteur totale 4 pieds, largeur 2 pieds 3 pouces.*

They sold for 498 *livres.* The buyer's name is poorly written in the margin of the sale catalogue, but it could be read as "Harcourt."

French (Paris); c. 1765
Height: 4' 5¼" (135.2 cm.)
Width: 2' (60.8 cm.)
Depth: 1' 4½" (41.9 cm.)
Accession number
81.DA.82.1-2

Veneered with ebony, kingwood, amaranth, and satinwood, with gilt bronze mounts.

63

This clock is a masterpiece of modeling, casting, chasing, and gilding. All the small decorative elements such as the garland of laurel around the face, the rosettes filling the trellis on the plinth, and the husks in the flutes of the support to the vase are cast together with the major elements they decorate, not made separately and attached as was the more usual practice. The figures representing Sidereal and Terrestrial Time (or Astronomy and Geography) are well modeled and must have been made by an accomplished sculptor. As is so often the case with objects made entirely of bronze, the clock does not bear the *bronzier's* name. In an inventory of the clockmaker Jean-André Lepaute, a similar clock is described as being modeled by the *ciseleur* Etienne Martincourt, and a drawing for this clock by Martincourt has recently been discovered.

The face and the movement of the clock are signed Charles Le Roy (b. 1709, master 1733, d. 1771). Le Roy worked in the rue St. Denis from 1748 to 1769, but little else is known of his life. He does not seem to have been related to the illustrious Julien Le Roy (see No. 9).

In a revolutionary inventory of royal possessions, a clock of the same model is described as belonging to Louis XVI:

> *No. 5: Une pendule en forme de vase ornée de deux figures rép-*
> *resentant l'astronomie et la géographie, le tout en cuivre doré et*
> *or moulu, le mouvement à sonnerie — 2 pieds de haut et 1 pied 6*
> *po de large — par Charles le Roi, Chez M. Robin.*

This would seem to indicate that the museum's clock was once in royal possession. Two other clocks of the same model exist in the Cooper-Hewitt Museum, New York, and a private collection; but they do not have movements by this maker.

The clock, as is the case with most of the clocks in the museum's collection, is in working order. It strikes on the hour and the half hour and the sound of the bell is perhaps the same as that heard by Louis XVI.

French (Paris); c. 1765

Height: 2′ 4″ (71.1 cm.)

Width: 1′ 11½″ (59.7 cm.)

Depth: 1′ ¾″ (32.4 cm.)

Accession number 73.DB.78

Gilded bronze.

This lidded bowl on a stand, known as an *écuelle,* is decorated with panels of blue and gold trellis. On the lid these panels are interrupted at intervals by four painted laurel leaf garlands containing an armorial, a monogram, and two rosettes. The handle of the lid is modeled and painted to resemble a branch with leaves and berries.

This *écuelle* is of soft paste porcelain; and both the bowl and the stand bear the crossed L's mark of the Sèvres porcelain manufactory, enclosing the date letter L for 1764. They also bear the mark of the porcelain painter Pierre-Antoine Méreaud *l'aîné,* who was active at Sèvres 1754-1791. He decorated a variety of pieces such as this in the early 1760's with varying rosette, shell, and scroll patterns set amongst gilding, often using the shades of red and blue found on this piece.

The armorial is that of an unmarried daughter of a King of France, while the monogram reads ML. The surviving sales records from Sèvres show that on the 24th of February 1764 *"1 Ecuelle et Plateau frize armoriée"* was delivered to Madame Louise, the eighth daughter of Louis XV. She paid the relatively high sum of 240 *livres* for this *écuelle,* which must have been specially ordered to be decorated with the armorial and monogram. This is the only piece of Sèvres porcelain that she is recorded to have purchased directly from the manufactory in 1764.

Madame Louise was born in Versailles on July 15th, 1737. When she was one year old, she was sent to live at the Abbey of Fontevrault, along with her sisters Marie-Thérèse-Félicité, Sophie, and Victoire. Madame Louise stayed in the Abbey for twelve years before returning to Versailles and the Court. A large commode by Gilles Joubert in the museum's collection (No. 30), was one of a pair delivered to her bedroom at Versailles in 1769. In the next year, however, she left the Court, on April 11th, to live the rest of her life in the Carmelite convent of Saint-Denis as Sister Thérèse of Saint Augustine. On her deathbed in December 1787, she was said to have uttered the words *"à Paradis! à Paradis! au grand galop"* — a reminder of her life at Court and a passion in her youth for hunting, a lifestyle that she had not known for the last seventeen years of her life.

French (Sèvres); 1764

Overall Height:
5″ (12.7 cm.)
Width of Bowl:
7¾″ (19.7 cm.)
Diameter of stand:
8¼″ (21 cm.)

Accession number
78.DE.65.a,b,c

Soft paste porcelain.

This cabinet is stamped, beneath the apron, JOSEPH for Joseph Baumhauer. We have already pointed out (p. 46) that Baumhauer died in 1772 after a long illness, and it is possible that this cabinet was made by his son, Gaspard Joseph Baumhauer, who took over his father's shop and probably continued to use his father's stamp.

The cabinet is in the early, severely architectonic neoclassical style, with its double canted fluted pilasters and Ionic capitals. Although there is no doubt that a fine cabinetmaker like Joseph would have been capable of making the piece, he would, after having been trained in and consistently worked in the rococo style, surely have found it difficult to produce such a novel, strictly linear form.

For all its apparent simplicity, the cabinet must have been an expensive commission. The large panels of Japanese lacquer date from the late seventeenth century and are made in a technique known as *kijimakie*. In this technique the wood itself is the exposed ground, and it has been sanded to heighten its strong grain. Only the elements of the design are of raised lacquer. Large panels in this technique are rarely found on French furniture of this period.

The top is not of the usual marble but yellow jasper, which is a rare refinement. The doors of the front open to reveal four drawers, the fronts of which are veneered with amaranth, while the side doors conceal shallow cupboards.

French (Paris); c. 1765

Height: 2′ 11⅜″ (89.7 cm.)
Width: 3′ 11¼″ (120.0 cm.)
Depth: 1′ 11⅛″ (58.7 cm.)

Accession number
79.DA.58

Veneered ebony and satinwood, with panels of Japanese lacquer and ebony, with gilt bronze mounts.

69

A drip pan of one of this set of six wall lights is signed '*Fait par Caffiery*', showing that they were made by the famous *bronzier* Philippe Caffiéri (1714-1774), the son of Jacques Caffiéri (b. 1678, master 1714, d. 1755). In an inventory of Philippe Caffiéri's stock, taken at his death in 1774, we find the following entry:

> *No. 94. Une paire de grands bras à trois branches en couleur avec des grandes Guirlandes de laurier agraphées dans les rouleaux des branches et nouées d'une draperie en noir de fumée avec un Vase dont le corps est aussi en noir de fumée.*

The wall lights described here, with their patinated bronze drapery and vases, exactly resemble a set of six in the Lazienski Palace in Warsaw. Caffiéri worked in Warsaw between 1766 and 1768 and doubtless provided works in gilt bronze for the palace. A drawing for this model, signed by Philippe Caffiéri, has recently been discovered.

The backs of the museum's wall lights bear the stenciled inventory number 151. It is possible that the set was once larger. Most large salons, suitable for lights of this size, would have been fitted with four mirrors, and each mirror would have been flanked by a pair of wall lights.

A drawing by Caffiéri for a sconce of similar design exists. It is not dated, but it is accompanied by a bill authorized for payment on March 20, 1767. It was part of a project for works in gilt bronze to be made for Nôtre Dame, Paris. Signed works by Philippe Caffiéri are rare. Both he and his father only occasionally signed their works, usually with just the surname "Caffiéri." The father's objects are always in the rococo style.

French (Paris); c. 1768-1770

Height: 2' 1½" (64.8 cm.)
Width: 1' 4" (40.7 cm.)
Depth: 11⅝" (29.6 cm.)

Accession numbers
78.DF.263.1-4;
82.DF.35.1-2.

Gilded bronze.

This set of four tapestries was woven at the Manufacture Royale des Gobelins between 1772 and 1773. They illustrate various scenes from Cervantes' *Don Quixote* and were woven after cartoons painted by Charles-Antoine Coypel (1694 - 1752). He produced twenty-eight paintings of this subject for sets of tapestries between 1714 and 1752. The elaborate surrounds and frames (known as the *alentours*) were redesigned from time to time as styles changed, and those found on this set are of the eighth and last design, made by Michel Audran and Pierre Cozette. They were used between 1763 and 1787.

The tapestry illustrated shows *Entrée de Sancho dans l'Ile de Barataria* (68); the three remaining hangings show *Don Quixotte guéri de sa folie par la Sages* (66), *Le Repas de Sancho, dans l'Ile de Barataria* (67), and *Poltronerie de Sancho à la Chasse* (69).

Numerous sets were woven from the Coypel paintings starting from early decades of the eighteenth century. The earlier tapestries were given yellow grounds. The strong crimson, woven in imitation of damask, became popular in the 1760's; and in this set it has, along with all the other colors of the wide variety of dyes used, remained extremely bright and relatively unfaded.

On the 19th of August 1786, the duc and duchesse of Saxe-Teschen visited the looms of the Manufacture des Gobelins. They were traveling in France under the name of the comte and comtesse de Bély. Albert-Casimir-Auguste de Saxe, duc de Teschen (1738-1822), was the sixth son of the Elector of Saxony, Frederick Augustus II. His wife, Marie-Christine, was the fourth daughter of the Empress Marie-Thérèse of Austria and sister of Queen Marie-Antoinette. It was, therefore, fitting that Louis XVI should give them, two days after their visit to the Gobelins, this set of tapestries. The tapestries remained in the possession of their descendants until 1936.

It is interesting to note that the set of tapestries discussed and illustrated as No. 38 was given by Louis XVI to the Grand Duke Paul of Russia and his wife, Maria Feodorovna, four years earlier in 1782. At the same time, he also gave them a set of four Don Quixote tapestries which still hang at the Palace of Pavlovsk, Leningrad. Such elaborate hangings were frequently presented to the crowned heads and the nobility of other countries in Europe as diplomatic gifts.

French (Gobelins); 1772-1773

66. Height: 12' 2" (370.8 cm.)
Width: 12' 10" (391.1 cm.)
67. Height: 12' 2" (370.8 cm.)
Width: 16' 5 ½" (501.6 cm.)
68. Height: 12' 2" (370.8 cm.)
Width: 13' 10" (421.6 cm.)
69. Height: 12' 2" (370.8 cm.)
Width: 13' 6" (411.4 cm.)

Accession numbers
82.DD.66-69

Silk and wool.

This secrétaire is of unique form. The central section of the front can be raised on an iron ratchet. It then opens out to make a large reading and writing surface. The fall fronts of most French secrétaires (see Nos. 39 and 41) lower to reveal nests of drawers and pigeon holes. This example is unusually low and would thus not have had a writing surface of sufficient size. It was probably designed for a library; and the surface provided by this unique mechanical method is wide enough to hold an open folio.

The secrétaire is attributed to Jean-François Leleu (b. 1729, master 1764, d. 1807). A secrétaire bearing the same gilt bronze mounts and distinctive trellis marquetry stamped with Leleu's name is in the Musée Nissim de Camondo, Paris, while a long cabinet, similarly decorated and stamped, is in the Château de Menars.

Leleu, together with Jean-Henri Riesener (see No. 41), was apprenticed to Jean-François Oeben (see No. 27). At Oeben's death in 1763, both Riesener and Leleu tried to win the hand of the widow Oeben, thus gaining the lucrative business and the probability of eventually becoming the royal cabinet-maker. The jealousy between these two rivals caused a number of fights, one of which required police intervention. Eventually Riesener prevailed, married the widow, and indeed did become the royal cabinetmaker in 1774.

Jean-François Leleu set out on his own, and throughout his work the influence of his master can be seen both in his marquetry and in his use of complicated mechanical arrangements. In this secrétaire only two of the eight small drawers above the rising front bear locks, which, when activated, lock the six small drawers between and above them at the same time. At the sides of the secrétaire are columns of four drawers, and again only the top drawer is fitted with a conventional lock. When the drawer is pushed in, it activates bolts in the interior carcase, which lock the drawers below.

The interior of the secrétaire is inscribed 1770, and it is in the early neoclassical style. The shape is severely rectilinear, and the mounts are fairly simple and restrained. Its beauty is in the marquetry and the mechanical fittings.

The secrétaire was formerly in the collection at Mentmore Towers and had probably belonged to the Rothschild family, those great collectors of French eighteenth-century art, since the late nineteenth century.

French (Paris); c. 1770

Height: 3' 6" (107 cm.)
Width: 3' 11" (119 cm.)
Depth: 1' 5¼" (43.6 cm.)

Accession number
82.DA.81

Oak veneered with satiné rouge, thuya, rosewood, tulipwood, ebony, and satinwood with gilt bronze mounts.

This set of four tapestries was made at the Manufacture des Gobelins. The central ovals show various scenes from classical mythology and are after paintings by François Boucher (1703-1770). The borders were designed by Maurice Jacques (c. 1712-1784) and Louis Tessier (1718/19-1781). The largest tapestry shows *Diana and Callisto and Vertumnus and Pomona* (469) (the painting for the latter by Boucher was made in 1763 and is now in the Musée du Louvre). The three smaller tapestries show *Venus and Vulcan* (466) (the painting is now in the Grand Trianon), *Venus on the Waters* (467), and *Aurora and Cephalus* (468) (the painting of 1765 is also in the Louvre).

In 1782 the set was given by Louis XVI to the Grand Duke of Russia, Paul Petrovich (who later became Czar Paul I) and his wife, Maria Feodorovna, who were traveling in Europe that year incognito as le comte et comtesse du Nord. The tapestries were installed in the Palace of Pavlovsk outside Leningrad, where they remained until they were sold in the early decades of the twentieth century by the Russian government to Lord Duveen.

Tapestries incorporating classical deities were extremely popular with the English nobility, and sets were made for William Weddel (Newby Hall), the Earls of Jersey (Osterly Park House), and Bradford (Weston Park), Sir Lawrence Dundas (Moore Park, now at Aske Hall), the Duke of Portland (Welbeck Abbey), and the Earl of Coventry (Croome Court). The last mentioned set is now in the Metropolitan Museum of Art, New York. In most cases the tapestries were made for rooms designed by Robert Adam and were woven to fit the walls of the rooms exactly. At Croome Court and Osterly Park House, they were made to fit around the mantelpiece, doors, and mirrors. Fire screens and chair covers were sometime ordered en suite, and the end result was harmonious if a little claustrophobic. The museum's tapestries would have been originally framed within wooden borders, a small blue *galon* or border having been specially provided for the use of nails.

French (Gobelins); 1776-1778

466. Height: 12' 5" (381 cm.) Width: 16' (487.7 cm.)

467. Height: 12' 6" (383.5 cm.) Width: 10' 4" (317.5 cm.)

468. Height: 12' 5" (381 cm.) Width: 10' 5" (322.5 cm.)

469. Height: 12' 6" (383.5 cm.) Width: 20' 5" (624.8 cm.)

Accession numbers 71.DD.466-469

Silk and wool.

The upright secrétaire (*secrétaire à abbatant*) began to be a fashionable form of furniture at the end of the first half of the eighteenth century. It probably took its shape from the earlier Spanish *vargueño,* though secrétaires do appear built into some English libraries of the late seventeenth century. The fall front lowers to form a writing surface, revealing drawers and pigeon holes.

This secrétaire is stamped M. CARLIN for Martin Carlin (master 1766, d. 1785). Carlin specialized in making furniture mounted with Sèvres porcelain plaques, and a number of secrétaires by him, decorated in this manner, exist in private and public collections such as the Metropolitan Museum of Art in New York and the James A. de Rothschild Collection at Waddesdon Manor in England. This form of decoration began about 1760 and within ten years became extremely fashionable. The *marchand-mercier* (see p. 46) Philippe Poirier had an almost complete monopoly with the Sèvres manufactory for these plaques, and in the Sèvres sales register his name appears with great frequency above long lists of plaques which were sold to him. He then commissioned cabinet-makers such as Martin Carlin and Adam Weisweiler to make furniture incorporating them. The plaques are often marked on their reverses with code letters for dates and with symbols for the painters, and in this way it is possible to date the secrétaires quite precisely. The two rectangular plaques on the fall front of the museum's secrétaire are dated with the letter Y for 1776, and two of the small plaques on the drawer front below are marked Z for 1777. One of the smaller plaques still bears its price label, showing that it cost 36 *livres*; and another bears the symbol for the painter Jean-Charles Sioux *l'ainé,* who worked at the Manufactory between 1752 and 1792. Unfortunately the fine large rectangular plaques do not bear painter's symbols.

This elegant secrétaire is unusually small and was probably made for a small *chambre à coucher* or *cabinet*. A secrétaire of similar form at the Metropolitan Museum of Art, New York, belonged to the actress Madame De Laguerre. It was sold after her death, in 1782, to Maria Feodorovna, who took it, with the tapestries illustrated in No. 38, to her palace of Pavlovsk, outside St. Petersburg.

French (Paris); c. 1777
Height: 3′ 6¼″ (104.8 cm.)
Width: 3′ 3¾″ (101 cm.)
Depth: 1′ 2″ (35.5 cm.)

Accession number
81.DA.80

Veneered with tulipwood, satinwood, amaranth, with satinwood and ebony stringing, with Sèvres soft paste porcelain plaques and gilt bronze mounts.

This cup and saucer is of a very popular shape, made at Sèvres from 1752, called a *gobelet litron et soucoupe*. The shape was made in five sizes, this example being of the second largest size. The brown ground color with elaborate raised gilding, enamel "jewels," and a painted polychrome scene are uncommon. The cup and saucer have ovals of porcelain enameled with cameo-style profile portraits. These are set into gold frames over solid ovals of tooled gold. The gilding consists partly of foils formed in steel dies which were specially made for the Sèvres Manufactory by the Parisian engraver Le Guay. These were ordered to be made up from designs by Jean-Baptiste-Etienne Genest, who was head of the artists' studio at Sèvres. Around this is raised gilding and, set into it, are globules of transparent and opaque enamels colored red, orange, green, and white, which imitate jewels and pearls.

The cup and saucer are both marked in blue beneath their bases with the crossed L's mark of the Sèvres Manufactory, enclosing the date letters DD for 1781. In addition both bear the triangular mark of the painter Capelle (active at Sèvres from 1746 until 1800). The saucer bears the initials LG in gold script for the gilder Etienne-Henry Le Guay. The cameo portraits are copied from designs made for the large soft paste porcelain dinner service commissioned from the Sèvres Manufactory in the 1770's by Catherine the Great of Russia. They depict, on the cup, Juno and Amon and, on the saucer, Jupiter Capitolinus and Omphale.

The brown ground color was not commonly used at Sèvres, though in the 1770's and 1780's many pieces, particularly cups and saucers, were made as gifts with unusual types of enameled decoration. This cup and saucer is thought not to have come from a tea service but rather to have been made as a gift or collector's piece, and at quite a considerable cost. The *Régistre des Peintres* of 1781 at Sèvres includes a ground color called *fond merde d'oie* which may well describe a color such as this. Other colors noted in the kiln records of 1781 as *fond marron* and *fond boue de Paris* might equally well describe this shade of brown.

French (Sèvres); 1781

Cup:
Height: 2¾" (6.9 cm.)
Width: 3¾" (9.4 cm.)
Saucer:
Height: 1⅓" (3.6 cm.)
Width: 5¼" (13.5 cm.)

Accession number
81.DE.28.a-b

Soft paste porcelain.

This secrétaire is not stamped with a maker's name, but it is securely attributed to the royal cabinetmaker Jean-Henri Riesener (b. 1734, master 1768, royal cabinetmaker 1774-1784, d. 1806). He was the most able, and perhaps the wealthiest, cabinetmaker of the second half of the eighteenth century. Riesener was apprenticed to Jean-François Oeben (see p. 72), an earlier royal cabinetmaker, and at Oeben's death married his widow, thereby securing for himself a prosperous workshop, a good clientele, and eventually, in 1774, the highest position of *ébéniste du roi*. After ten years of producing a prodigious amount of extremely elaborate and expensive furniture for the Crown, his dismissal from the position in 1784 was due partly to a realization by the King that economies were needed, and that such "conspicuous consumption" was not looked upon with much favor by the people of France.

Although the museum's secrétaire has not been found in the royal inventories, it is of the same high quality as other pieces made by Riesener for Marie-Antoinette and the Court. The mounts are finely chased in their smallest details, and the construction of the piece is extremely fine throughout. The entire interior fittings, made of solid mahogany, can be pulled out from the front to reveal secret lidded compartments in the deeper recesses of the piece.

The secrétaire has an interesting provenance. It was acquired at the sale of George Watson Taylor in 1832 by Alexander, 10th Duke of Hamilton. It stood in the Duke's dressing room together with a secrétaire and a commode en suite, made by Riesener for the Château de Saint Cloud (both now in the Metropolitan Museum of Art, New York). It was sold at the famous Hamilton Palace sale in 1882 for the then high price of £5,460 to the dealer Wertheimer, who was acting as agent for Cornelis Vanderbilt. It was acquired by the museum at the sale of the possessions of Vanderbilt's daughter, Countess Szechenyi.

French (Paris); c. 1780

Height: 5' 1" (154.9 cm.)
Width: 3' 8½" (113 cm.)
Depth: 1' 6⅜" (46.6 cm.)

Accession number
71.DA.104

Veneered with panels of Japanese lacquer and ebony, with gilt bronze mounts.

On the white marble plinth of the clock stand two bronze Vestal Virgins, one of whom pours a libation over the flame which constantly burned in the Temple of Vesta, the Roman goddess of the Hearth. In relief around the white marble altar, which contains the clock movement, is a procession of gilt bronze figures and animals, who are preparing for a sacrifice to the goddess. A spray of gilt bronze flowers serves as a pointer to the time, which may be read on the revolving enameled and jeweled rings.

This classical theme is found on a number of other clocks — at least five of this form are known to exist in private and public collections. In this late eighteenth century model, all traditional semblance of a clock is gone; and the object takes the form of a piece of decorative sculpture, its basic function not being obvious at first glance. The name of the maker of the movement is not known, but it is possible to attribute the bronzes of the clock to Pierre-Philippe Thomire (1751-1843), the foremost *bronzier* of the last decades of the eighteenth and the early nineteenth centuries. A number of Thomire's works are signed or documented, and in them we find many elements similar to those found on this piece.

A watercolor drawing at the Musée des Arts Décoratifs in Paris shows this model of clock standing on a mantelpiece, together with candelabra and various small decorative objects, with firedogs below. The drawing is attributed to Jean-Démosthène Dugourc (1749-1825), a well-known designer whose work was always in the refined neoclassical style. Some of the objects in the drawing — one of the firedogs and one of the small decorative objects standing near the clock — exist, and they are known to have been made after models by the sculptor Louis-Simon Boizot (1743-1809). It is possible that it was he who made the figures of the Virgins.

French (Paris); c. 1785

Height: 1' 8⅞" (53 cm.)
Width: 2' 1⅛" (63.4 cm.)
Depth: 9¼" (23.5 cm.)

Accession number 82.DB.2

Marble with gilded and patinated bronze, with jeweled and enameled dials.

One of the panels is painted with the monograms LSX and MJL, which almost certainly must be for Louis-Stanislas-Xavier, the comte de Provence (who became Louis XVIII in 1814), and his wife Marie-Joséphine-Louise (1753–1810), the eldest daughter of Victor Amadeus III of Sardinia.

The six silk panels are beautifully painted, with extraordinary attention given to minute details. The artist is not known, but the panels resemble not only painted wooden panels still found lining the walls of the *salons* of great Parisian hôtels but also, and perhaps more closely, the classical wall papers produced by the manufactory of Réveillon. One paper in particular may be singled out, produced in 1785 and designed by Jean-Baptiste Fay. On it we see the same type of basket filled with similar flowers, standing on a plinth bearing piled up musical instruments, and a panel showing children playing, painted to resemble a Wedgwood blue and white plaque. All these elements are found in the museum's panels. These careful paintings, highlighted in gold, seem not to be mere models for wall paper but were probably produced by the same artists who worked in this style for the manufactory.

Two other silk panels, apparently en suite with those in the museum, are in the Musée des Arts Décoratifs, Paris, and another passed through the Paris market in the 1930's.

In 1784 Jacques-François Chalgrin (1739–1811) built a small Pavillon de Musique in the garden which surrounded the comtesse de Provence's Château de Montreuil. Though the château has been destroyed, the Pavillon still stands. The decoration of the rooms of the building reflects the surrounding gardens, and the main rotunda is completely painted in trompe-l'oeil with a garden. Another octagonal room, which once had five pairs of windows giving access to the *jardin anglais*, has narrow strips of mirror set into its walls. It is plausible that the mirrors replace these silk panels, whose decoration would have been echoed by the stucco garlands of flowers supporting blue and white cameos bearing M's above the windows.

French (Paris); c. 1785

Height: 4' 9" (144.8 cm.)
Width: 7" (17.8 cm.)

Accession number
73.DH.89.1-6

Silk painted with gouache, with gold paint; the gilded frames (not shown) are not contemporary. A detail of one of the six panels is illustrated.

44. DESK

This massive desk, standing on twelve legs, was made in Germany by one of the ablest cabinetmakers of the eighteenth century, David Roentgen (b. 1743, master 1780, d. 1807). Roentgen maintained a large workshop at Neuwied-on-the-Rhine, which had been set up earlier in the century by his equally famous father, Abraham. He sold his furniture to courts throughout Europe and was patronized by Catherine the Great, who much admired his work. He also established a shop in Paris where he was forced to become a member of the guild of *ébénistes* in 1780. His furniture, which at the beginning of his career had a confused Franco-German style, eventually became severely neoclassical. He specialized in large carcase pieces, and his tables, commodes, desks, and secrétaires often had very complicated mechanical fittings which were made by his colleague Peter Kinzing. Roentgen is famous for his pictorial marquetry, in which he did not use scorching for shading but arranged small pieces of wood in various shades to achieve the same effect.

The museum's roll-top desk has a typically complicated mechanical fitting. The interior, behind the roll top, has numerous drawers which spring open at the pressure of concealed buttons and levers. In the superstructure, behind the large gilt bronze plaque, is a contraption of many parts that moves out and opens at the turn of a key. It contains a folding reading stand and side "wings" of compartments with mechanically opening tops, one of which contains an inkwell and sand pot, with small drawers below. At the back of the desk is a removable panel for access to the movement.

The desk once belonged to Count Janos Palffy of Vienna, but its earlier history is not known. It is reputed to have been the desk on which the Louisiana Purchase was signed in 1803 at the Château de Malmaison, but there is no documentary evidence to prove this, nor does it appear in the Malmaison inventories.

A desk of the same model, but with a different gilt bronze plaque, was until recently in a Parisian private collection. Another very similar desk that formerly belonged to Catherine the Great is now in the Hermitage Museum, Leningrad, together with a considerable number of other pieces by this great cabinetmaker.

German (Neuwied); c. 1780-1785

Height: 5′ 5″ (165.1 cm.)
Width: 4′ 11⅛″ (150.3 cm.)
Depth: 2′ 9½″ (85.1 cm.)

Accession number 72.DA.47

Veneered with mahogany, with gilt bronze mounts.

This elegant assemblage of oriental porcelain and gilt bronze was probably designed to function as a *jardinière* and would have been placed on a stand or table. Another of identical form is in the British Royal Collection. It was acquired by the Prince Regent (later George IV) from Thomire et Cie. and was delivered to Carlton House in 1812. It stands today in Windsor Castle.

The museum's vase was acquired from Count Alfred Potocki. The vase was reputedly bought at the Revolutionary sales in Paris by his great-great-grandmother Princess Isabella Lubomirska (1736-1816), who was a cousin of King Stanislas of Poland. She traveled continuously in Europe between 1785 and 1791 and stayed in the Palais Royal in 1786. She was a good friend of Marie-Antoinette. It is quite plausible that she did indeed acquire the vase at the dispersal of the royal collections, for when she finally returned to her estates at Lancut in Poland, she brought twenty coachloads of French furniture with her. Unfortunately her name cannot be found among the buyers at the Revolutionary sales, but it is of course likely that she used an agent to bid for her.

The vase at Windsor may also have been purchased at the Revolutionary sales by Pierre-Philippe Thomire (1751-1843), who originally made the mounts. The style of the mounts conforms closely to Thomire's early work, and elements such as the vine leaves, grapes, and curling ribbed horns are found on other works documented to him.

The large Chinese bowl is covered with a powder blue glaze known in France as *bleu soufflé* because the powdered color was blown onto the vase through a bamboo tube.

The mounts:
French (Paris); c. 1780-1785
The ceramic:
Chinese (Qianlong);
c. 1730-1750

Height: 2' 7½" (80 cm.)
Diameter: 1' 10½"
(57.2 cm.)

Accession number
70.DI.115

Porcelain, marble, and gilt bronze.

The settee and the four armchairs are stamped TILLIARD for Jean-Baptiste Tilliard II (master 1752, d. 1797). He was the son of Jean-Baptiste I who retired in 1764 at the age of seventy-eight. They both used the same stamp as was often the custom with father and son practising the same craft. Pieces in the rococo style are therefore to be credited to the father, while those in the neoclassical style, such as this set of furniture, were made by the son.

The settee and chairs are typical of Tilliard's work, being richly and well carved but somewhat lacking in gracefulness. The set would originally have included many more pieces, and the massive quality suggests that it was made for a large *salon*. Another armchair from the set is in the Cleveland Museum of Art.

French (Paris); c. 1775

Settee:
Height: 3' 11⅜" (120.3 cm.)
Width: 7' 6½" (229.7 cm.)
Depth: 3' ½" (92.7 cm.)

Armchairs:
Height: 3' 5" (101.6 cm.)
Width: 2' 5" (73.6 cm.)
Depth: 2' 5½" (74.9 cm.)

Accession number
78.DA.99.1–5

Gilded oak; the velvet upholstery modern.

It is almost certain that this *chaise de toilette* is from a set of seat furniture made by Georges Jacob (b. 1739, master 1765, d. 1814) in 1787 for Marie-Antoinette's *chambre à coucher du Treillage* at the Petit Trianon. The set for the trelliswork bedroom originally consisted of two armchairs, two side chairs, a screen, a footstool (all returned to the Trianon in 1942), and a bed, a settee, and a swivel chair.

The museum's chair appears to be the missing *chaise de toilette*. It swivels on wooden rollers, and the back is low for the dressing of hair, without the cresting of pine cones and floral wreaths found on the other chairs of the set. Unfortunately the chair has been stripped of its polychrome paint. The rest of the set is painted in naturalistic colors, the flowers (lily of the valley and jasmine) are white and their leaves and stalks, green; while the wheat ears and carved "caning" are yellow on a pale blue ground. The existing documents show that the elaborate and extremely delicate carving was by Rode and Jean-Philibert Triquet and the painting by Chaillot de Prusse. Some pieces of the set at the Trianon are stamped G. JACOB; but, as was usually the case, this only shows that the set was made in his workshop, under his direction, but by the hands of a number of other skilled craftsmen.

Jacob was frequently commissioned by the Crown and his output between his mastership and the Revolution was prolific. During and after the Revolution, with the support of the painter David, he remained in favor. His descendants continued to produce fine work until 1847.

French (Paris); c. 1787

Height: 2' 9½" (85.1 cm.)
Width: 1' 10¾" (57.8 cm.)
Depth: 1' 9½" (54.6 cm.)

Accession number
72.DA.51

Carved oak, with caning; the velvet upholstery modern.

95

48. WINE BOTTLE COOLER

This wine bottle cooler comes from the celebrated dinner service ordered from the Sèvres Manufactory by Louis XVI in 1783 for his use at Versailles. The production of the service was scheduled to take from 1783 until 1805 due to the quantity of work involved and the immense cost of each element. There were to be twenty-four wine coolers of this size in the service, which was intended to consist of four hundred and forty-five pieces when completed.

With the execution of the King in 1793, the production of this service came to a halt. One hundred and ninety-seven pieces of the service were completed, of which the largest surviving group is in the British Royal Collection.

This wine cooler does not bear any date or decorators' marks. However, it is thought to be one of two recorded in the Sèvres Manufactory's sale records of 1790. The painted decoration is attributed to Charles-Eloi Asselin (active at Sèvres from 1765), who was one of the seven painters known to have been entrusted with the elaborate enameled scenes on these pieces. The dinner service has a dark blue (*bleu nouveau*) ground color with intricate gilding in arabesque patterns of flowers and foliage, with chased and burnished moldings around the painted reserves.

The painted decoration on this service involved so much work from the artists that it was one of the most expensive ever produced at the Sèvres Manufactory. This piece, called a *seau à bouteille ordinaire*, cost the King 960 *livres*, when most clients — even royal clients — were paying 200 to 220 *livres* for a *seau* of this size with even quite lavish decoration. The service was decorated with mythological scenes in the painted reserves, including illustrations of Ovid's *Métamorphoses* and Fénelon's *Aventures de Télémaque*. The scene shown in the illustration is taken from an engraving by Georg Haas after a painting by Jean-Baptiste-Marie Pierre (1713-1804) entitled *Hercule et Diomède*.

French (Sèvres); 1790

Height: 7⅓" (18.9 cm.)
Width: 10⅛" (25.8 cm.)

Accession number
82.DE.5

Soft paste porcelain.

This pair of wine bottle coolers, called *seaux à bouteilles ordinaires*, are of the same form as that shown in No. 48. They are marked with the crossed L's of the Sèvres porcelain manufactory surmounted by a crown; this indicates that they are made of hard paste porcelain — true porcelain. Hard paste porcelain is made with kaolin, a type of clay that was not discovered in France until 1769. Without kaolin the Sèvres manufactory had been making only an imitation of true porcelain called "soft paste." Hard paste wares were not produced in very large quantities at Sèvres until the end of the eighteenth century, though they completely replaced the use of soft paste in the course of the nineteenth century.

These wine coolers bear the date letters OO for 1792 and are decorated with gold and platinum on a black ground. The black ground is composed of a mixture of oxides of iron, copper, cobalt, and manganese. This decoration of gold and platinum on black became popular in the 1790's. These *seaux* bear the mark of the gilder Jean-Jacques Dieu. This scheme of decoration is not a reintroduction of the theme of chinoiserie, so popular in the rococo period, however, but an attempt to imitate oriental lacquer in another medium.

The pieces of Sèvres porcelain known with this black ground color are chiefly ornamental vases and wares for dinner services. The most complete service survives in the Hermitage Museum in Leningrad. It was bought by Prince Nikolay Borisovich Yusupov (1750-1831) and is date marked for 1791-1792. It is not known for whom the museum's *seaux* were made.

French (Sèvres); 1792
Height: 6½" (16.5 cm.)
Width: 9½" (23.5 cm.)

Accession number
72.DE.53.1-2

Hard paste porcelain.

The large blue enameled globe is studded with gilt stars and encircled by the signs of the zodiac in gilt bronze. The branches and griffins bear candleholders for eighteen lights.

An interesting document was recently discovered in the French archives. It was written in 1820 by Monsieur Galle, a *fondeur-doreur* who had provided work in gilt bronze both for Louis XVI and for Napoleon and the Emperor's numerous relatives. At the Restoration Galle offered to the Garde Meuble de la Couronne of Louis XVIII works that he had made for the various Paris Expositions and earlier, among which was the following:

"Lustre à poisson, au milieu d'un globe émaillé en bleu et parsemé d'étoiles est un cercle avec les signes du zodiaque et six griffons portant des lumières. De six patères placés entre chaque griffon partent douze branches ornées de ciselure; des ornements de bon goût en arabesque supportent l'anneau destiné à pendre le lustre; au dessous du cercle sur lequel sont placées les lumières six branches légères ornées d'enroulements suspendent une cuvette en cristal garnie d'une riche galerie et qui se termine par un culot dans lequel est placé sans être vu un bouchon destiné à renouveller l'eau que l'on place dans la cuvette avec les petits poissons rouges dont le mouvement continu récrée l'oeil agréablement. hauter du lustre 4. Pieds, diamètre 2. Pieds II P°. ce lustre à été exposé.
. . . .*3000   2400[livres]"*

As no chandelier of this model is found recorded in the French royal collections, it seems that the officials of the Garde Meuble were not intrigued by this whimsical object. But nonetheless it seems to have been a popular model, for a number still exist. One, in the Swedish Royal collection, is more profusely mounted with glass drops, showing that the museum's example has been somewhat denuded. Another, lacking all its drops, passed through the French art market in the 1970's.

Some of the elements of the chandelier — the griffins and the large rosetted scrolls above the glass bowl — appear in an engraving for a chandelier in Percier and Fontaines' *Recueil de décorations intérieurs* published in 1801.

French (Paris); c. 1810-1815
Height: 4' 3" (129.5 cm.)
Width: 3' 2" (96.5 cm.)

Accession Number
73.DH.76

Enameled metal, glass, and gilt bronze.

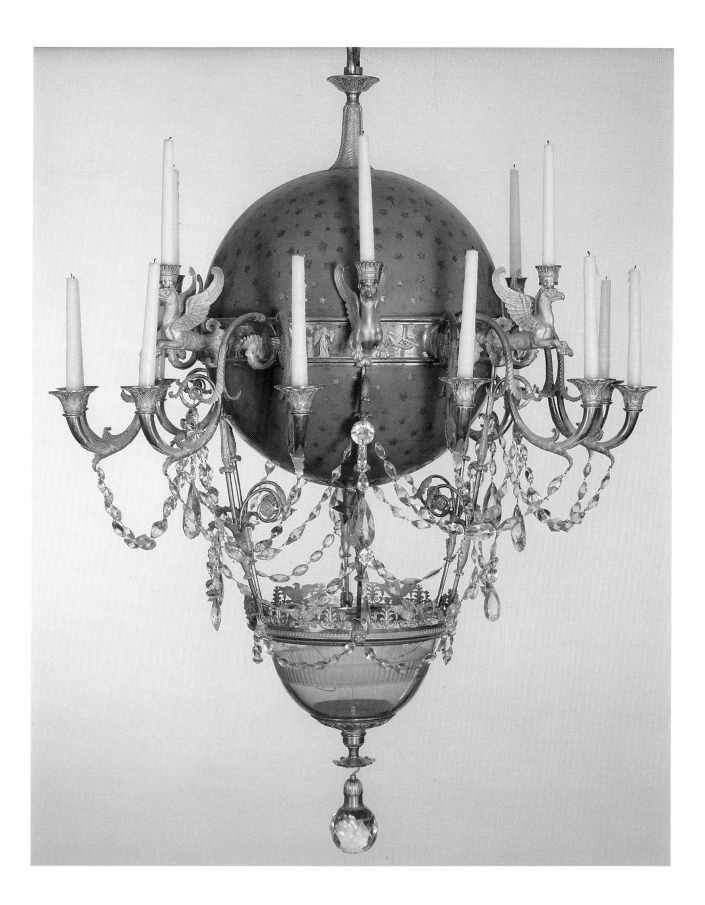

NO. 1 (p. 2)

NO. 18. A large new carpet from Savonnerie with a brown ground, strewn with large white scrolls and flowers in natural colors, having in the middle an oval cartouche in which there is a garland of flowers with a sunflower at its center, in a border also with a brown ground with baskets and vases of flowers, Length 7 *aunes* ½, width 3 *aunes* ⅔.

Note on measurements:
a *ligne* is 2 mm. (⅛"),
a *pouce* is 2.7 cm. (1 1/16"),
a *pied* is 32.4 cm. (12 11/16"),
an *aune* is 1.19m. (3' 10⅞").

NO. 4 (p. 8)

No. 122. A table with an ebony ground with compartments of white wood in the form of branches of oak leaves, covered with marquetry of flowers and birds in woods of different colors, the feet and the capitals of the legs of gilt copper.

Nos. 162, 163. Two tables of tortoiseshell with compartments of flowers and birds of wood marquetry of different natural colors outlined in ivory, with columnar legs of which the bases, astragals, and capitals are of gilt copper.

NO. 6 (p. 12)

6. A marquetry cabinet in the form of a sarcophagus of which the ground is of tortoiseshell, brass, and pewter, fitted with six fluted bands of gilt copper decorated above with female heads and below with lions' muzzles. Height of three *pieds* nine *pouces,* length of sixteen *pouces* eleven *lignes,* and depth of thirteen *pouces.*

NO. 8 (p. 16)

No. 194. Hangings of the Chariot: Four tapestries of low warp, wool and silk, made at the Gobelins, designed by Le Brun, representing in the middle the arms and the device of Louis XIV in a cartouche carried on a Triumphal Chariot, accompanied by trophies of arms; the border is a guilloche which encloses fleurs-de-lys and bronze colored roses, each hanging is 2 *aunes* ½ in width and 2 *aunes* ⅚ in length.

NO. 17 (p. 34)

No. 163. In the salon with the fireplace are [a set of] fire dogs, which represent two sphinxes, one of which is playing with a cat and the other with a monkey, mounted on two feet, of the grandest style. Connoisseurs will notice that these sphinxes are not designed like those that are normally made for fire dogs; these can be considered as of the best design in France, fitted with hooks [supports?] gilded with ground gold.

NO. 19 (p. 38)

No. 132. A commode with four legs with a marble top of Breche violette, the bronzes representing two children who rasp snuff; in the middle is a monkey who powders himself with the snuff, gilded with ground gold.

NO. 30 (p. 60)

28 August 1769
Delivered by Mr. Joubert
For use in the bedroom of Madame Louise of France at the Château of Versailles.

No. 2556. Two commodes in the Régence manner [i.e. deep commodes with shaped fronts on short legs] of rosewood veneered in trelliswork, having in front two large drawers locking with a single key and on the sides two locking cupboards with a shelf inside, the panels ornamented throughout with small rosettes, the sides with two busts of women crowned with laurel, carried on two tapering pedestals with trelliswork and the keyhole surrounds, buttons, frames, fillets, rosettes, pendants, and feet shod with lions' paws, the whole very richly chased and gilded bronze with their marble tops of which one [is] griotte d'Italie [an Italian marble splashed with red and brown spots like Morello cherries] and the other d'Antin [marble from Antin], five and a half *pieds* long by 24 *pouces* deep and 34 *pouces* high.

NO. 31 (p. 62)

Lot 238. Two very rich corner cupboards in the form of a tapering pedestal with an ebony ground, ornamented with garlands, rosettes, and friezes of gilt bronze: the rest of the front is veneered with palissander. They are covered with white marble two *pouces* thick. Total height 4 *pieds,* width 2 *pieds* 3 *pouces.*

NO. 32 (p. 64)

No. 5. A clock in the shape of a vase decorated with two figures representing Astronomy and Geography, entirely in gilt bronze [with] striking movement—2 *pieds* high and 1 *pied* 6 *pouces* wide—by Charles le Roi, at Monsieur Robin's.

Note: It is probable that at the time this inventory was taken the clock was with Robin the clockmaker.   G.W.

NO. 35 (p. 70)

No. 94. A pair of large wall lights with three arms in [natural bronze] color with large garlands of laurel caught up in the scrolls of the arms and knotted with a drapery in smoky black [patina] with a vase of which the body is also in smoky black.

Note: *En couleur* is probably an abbreviation of the usual phrase *mis en couleur d'or* meaning that the bronze was dipped in acid to brighten it and then lacquered. This frequently was done instead of gilding.   G.W.

NO. 50 (p. 100)

Fish chandelier, in the middle of a blue enameled globe scattered with stars is a circle with the signs of the zodiac and six griffons carrying lights. From six paterae placed between each griffon spring twelve branches decorated with chasing: arabesque ornaments in good taste carry the ring intended to hang the chandelier: below the circle on which are placed the lights, six slender branches decorated with scrolls suspend a glass bowl garnished with a rich gallery and which is furnished with a metal piece in which is placed, without being visible, a plug intended for the removal of the water which one places in the bowl with small gold fish whose continuous movement will give agreeable recreation to the eye. Height of chandelier 4 *pieds,* diameter 2 *pieds* 2 *pouces.* This chandelier has been exhibited.

. . . . 3000   2400 livres

SELECT BIBLIOGRAPHY

Bellaigue, Geoffrey de, *The James A. De Rothschild Collection at Waddesdon Manor: Furniture, Clocks, and Gilt Bronzes,* two volumes, Fribourg, Office du Livre, 1974.

Brunet, Marcelle and Tamara Préaud, *Sèvres, des origines à nos jours,* Fribourg, Office du Livre, 1978.

Dauterman, Carl C., James Parker and Edith Appleton Standen, *Decorative Art from the Samuel H. Kress Collection at the Metropolitan Museum of Art,* London, Phaidon Press, 1964.

Eriksen, Svend, *Early Neo-Classicism in France,* London, Faber and Faber Ltd, 1974.

Verlet, Pierre, *French Royal Furniture,* London, Barrie and Rockliff, 1963.

Verlet, Pierre, *Le Mobilier Royal Français. Meubles de la Couronne Conservés en France,* two volumes, Paris, Editions d'Art et d'Histoire, 1945-1963.

Verlet, Pierre, *Les Meubles Français du XVIIIè Siècle,* Paris, Presses Universitaires de France, 1982.

Watson, Francis J.B., *Wallace Collection Catalogues, Furniture,* London, 1956.

Watson, Francis J.B., *Louis XVI Furniture,* London, A. Tiranti, 1960.

Watson, Francis J.B. and Carl C. Dauterman, *The Wrightsman Collection,* four volumes, New York, The Metropolitan Museum of Art, 1964 and 1970.

Wilson, Gillian B., *French Eighteenth Century Clocks in the J. Paul Getty Museum,* Malibu, The J. Paul Getty Museum, 1976.

INDEX

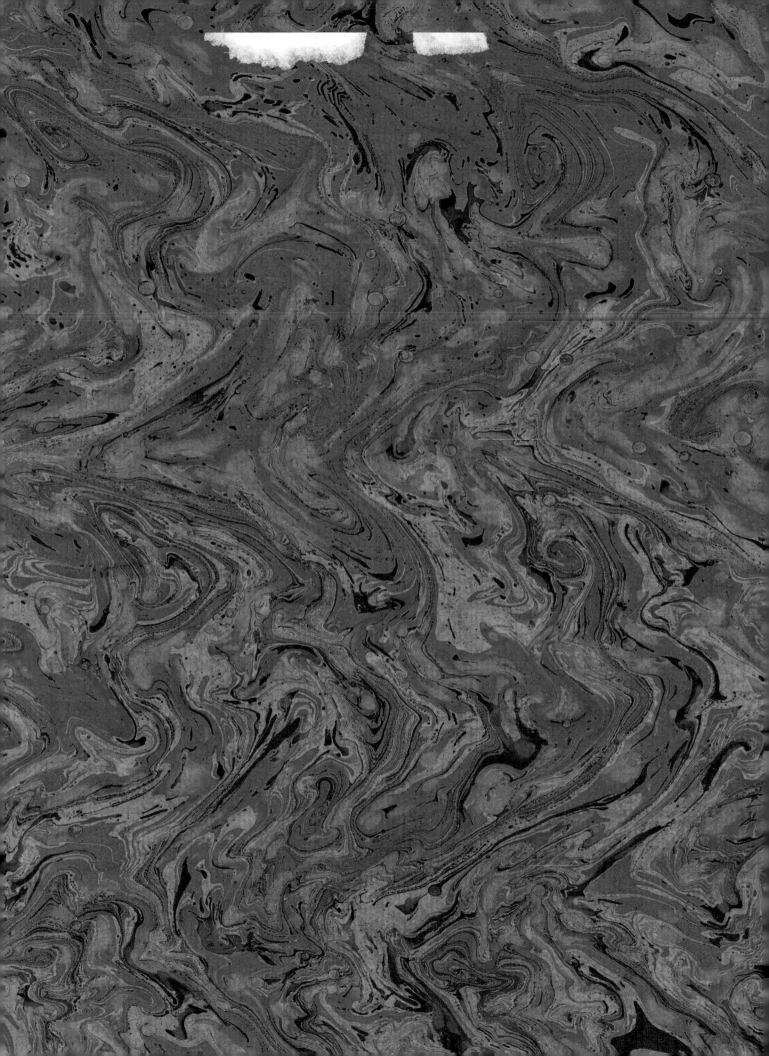